M000307726

# MANAGEMENT AS A CALLING

# MANAGEMENT AS A CALLING

LEADING BUSINESS, SERVING SOCIETY

Andrew J. Hoffman

STANFORD BUSINESS BOOKS
*An Imprint of Stanford University Press*
Stanford, California

© 2021 by the Board of Trustees of the Leland Stanford Junior University. All rights reserved.

No part of this book may be reproduced or transmitted in any form or by any means, electronic or mechanical, including photocopying and recording, or in any information storage or retrieval system without the prior written permission of Stanford University Press.

Special discounts for bulk quantities of Stanford Business Books are available to corporations, professional associations, and other organizations. For details and discount information, contact the special sales department of Stanford University Press. Tel: (650) 725-0820, Fax: (650) 725-3457

Printed in the United States of America on acid-free, archival-quality paper
Library of Congress Cataloging-in-Publication Data
Names: Hoffman, Andrew J., 1961- author.
Title: Management as a calling : leading business, serving society / Andrew J. Hoffman.
Description: Stanford, California : Stanford Business Books, an imprint of Stanford University Press, 2021. | Includes bibliographical references and index.
Identifiers: LCCN 2020035357 (print) | LCCN 2020035358 (ebook) | ISBN 9781503614802 (paperback) | ISBN 9781503615304 (epub)
Subjects: LCSH: Social responsibility of business. | Industrial management--Moral and ethical aspects. | Industrial management--Environmental aspects.
Classification: LCC HD60 .H633 2021 (print) | LCC HD60 (ebook) | DDC 658.4/08--dc23
LC record available at https://lccn.loc.gov/2020035357
LC ebook record available at https://lccn.loc.gov/2020035358

Cover design: Kevin Barrett Kane

Typeset by Kevin Barrett Kane in 10/14 Minion Pro

*To Joanne*

# CONTENTS

# TABLE AND FIGURES

# FOREWORD

On September 23rd, 2019, I was part of a small group of journalists escorted into the General Assembly hall at the United Nations headquarters in New York to watch world leaders and business executives announce plans for saving the planet and its 7.7 billion human inhabitants from climate change. The event was called to address the fact that with only a decade or so left to stabilize global temperature rise at a relatively safe 1.5 degrees Celsius, humankind is releasing greenhouse gas emissions into the atmosphere at record levels. "The climate emergency is a race we are losing, but it is a race we can win," Secretary-General António Guterres said. "But it will require fundamental transformations in all aspects of society—how we grow food, use land, fuel our transport and power our economies."[1]

But instead of action, I watched French president Emmanuel Macron, German chancellor Angela Merkel, Microsoft co-founder Bill Gates, New York billionaire Michael Bloomberg, and a revolving A-list of global powerbrokers fail to acknowledge the root cause of our crisis: an economic system predicated on endless profits, growth, and consumption without any regard for the consequences. The only person who seemed willing to point this out was a sixteen-year-old from Sweden. "We are in the beginning of a mass extinction. And all you can talk about is money and fairytales of eternal economic growth," Greta Thunberg told the room, barely holding back tears. "How dare you? If you choose to fail us, I say we will never forgive you."[2]

Thunberg's words sounded lonely and radical. But watching her face contort with anger while the CEOs and politicians she addressed smiled nervously and applauded, I realized I was observing a central faultline of our era: a younger generation demanding radical changes to address the crises caused by our global economic system and the older people in power unable or unwilling to make those changes.

For people who grew up in the shockwaves of 2008, my generation, her distrust of the status quo is practically mainstream. That was the conclusion that Deloitte reached in 2019 after polling more than thirteen thousand people under the age of forty around the world.[3] "Millennials and Gen Zs are disillusioned," reads a report summarizing the data. "They're not particularly satisfied with their lives, their financial situations, their jobs, government and business leaders, social media, or the way their data is used." Survey respondents cited climate change as their number one personal concern, followed by income inequality and unemployment. They did not appear to have much faith in the ability of business to fix these challenges or even to provide the conditions for a stable life. "We have less trust in employers because so many of our parents did lose their jobs, and they had been loyal to companies," one millennial told Deloitte. "We have less trust in the stock market because it crashed. And I think that a lot of us are worried that it is going to happen again."

I know this tension all too well, having graduated from journalism school in 2008, which was about the worst possible timing to embark on a new career. So bad, in fact, that *Business Insider* labeled the following year, "The year the newspaper died." When I reached out to a magazine editor with whom I'd interned to see if he knew of any jobs, I learned that he'd recently quit the industry for good. On his way out the door he gave an interview claiming there was "no future" for journalists like me. I feel lucky, having been able to intern at a small digital outlet in Vancouver, Canada, called *The Tyee* and then becoming a lead reporter on climate change, freelancing for outlets such as *VICE* and the *New York Times* and writing a book called *Are We Screwed?* (Bloomsbury, 2017)— but the feelings of precarity have never left.

It is this sense of precarity and disillusionment that lead so many twenty- and thirty-year-olds to rally behind politicians like Bernie Sanders and Elizabeth Warren, expressing support for an economy-transforming Green New Deal on climate change, demanding greater taxes on the rich, or telling public opinion researchers that they're interested in alternatives to capitalism (even if they can't quite define what exactly those are). This is not to say that every Millennial and Gen Z'er is a Molotov-hurling socialist. Many of them are simply freaked out by escalating climate chaos and Great Gatsby levels of inequality, and they are eager for bold and systemic solutions.

This is the context into which this book speaks, arguing that today's business students are in a unique position to provide those solutions—but only if they choose to. For decades, future executives have been taught to focus on short-term material gains and not worry about who or what is collateral damage in the process. Young people now entering or enrolled in business school face immense pressure to follow in that path. But if they do, society's crises will only get worse. Which is why Andrew Hoffman thinks "tomorrow's business leaders should be taught to do something that previous generations rarely did: they must start thinking critically about the role of business in society, their role as a manager in guiding those businesses, and the overall system in which they will practice their craft—capitalism."

This challenge isn't just for students looking to embark on a fuller and more meaningful career than one driven solely by the pursuit of money and status. It's for the business people and leaders who are already wielding power in our society, the business schools that train them, and anyone else who cares about creating a more equitable and environmentally sustainable world for everyone. We are in the midst of turbulent and distressing times, that much is plain to see. But the book in your hands provides an invaluable guide for navigating them. I hope that you respond to this book's challenge with the creativity and urgency it requires. Indeed, you must, because the future of my generation and all future generations is depending on it.

*Geoff Dembicki*
New York, 2020

# MANAGEMENT AS A CALLING

# CHAPTER 1

# MANAGEMENT AS A CALLING

OVER THE YEARS I have begun to question the business education we are giving to young people. This has been a gradual process, but two incidents stand out to me vividly as emblematic of my concerns. The first involved WorldCom CEO Bernie Ebbers, who in 2005 was convicted of fraud and conspiracy and sentenced to a twenty-five-year prison term. It was the largest accounting scandal in US history (until Bernie Madoff's Ponzi scheme was uncovered in 2008). I remember Ebbers's sentencing well, because I had just joined the faculty at the University of Michigan's Business School and was struck by the fact that no one was talking about it. Ebbers was a man who would have been held up as a model of success for our students, building the second-largest long-distance phone company in the country. But now he was a disgrace. It was not until the end of the day that the silence was finally broken. I walked onto an elevator and overheard a memorable conversation between two senior colleagues of mine: "What do you think of the Ebbers sentence?" one professor asked. "I think it's ridiculous," the colleague replied. "It's not like he killed someone."

The second happened four years later and involved an executive from General Motors who had come to the University of Michigan in search of a new position. GM had just been bailed out by the government; Frederick ("Fritz") Henderson had been named CEO, but many thought that his role was merely that of "interim" CEO and his term would be brief. As a result, some of his staff had begun to look for escape plans. When this executive interviewed with several faculty, including me, he said something that really struck me. He said with a smile that he had been at GM for thirty years and "really had a ball."

To me, the Ebbers incident speaks to how we as a society do not hold business people accountable; it illustrates the disconnect between the power that business executives possess and the responsibility that comes with that power. Ebbers did not commit actual murder, but he caused extraordinary hardship and pain for the company's employees, customers, suppliers, buyers, and investors, who lost millions of dollars because of his actions. WorldCom's stock lost 90 percent of its value in days, dropping from 83 cents to 6 cents per share, and its Chapter 11 filing made it the largest bankruptcy in history. Many legal experts have deemed the sentence fair.[1]

The GM executive incident illustrates how business people don't even hold themselves accountable. I was amazed that this executive could say that he was part of the leadership team that almost destroyed GM and that he enjoyed it. It was like a doctor coming out of an operating room where your parent is undergoing surgery and telling you that he had botched the operation, your parent almost died, someone else had to take over, but he "really had a ball" while it lasted.

## CRITIQUES OF BUSINESS AND BUSINESS EDUCATION

I am not alone in questioning how business leadership is being practiced in the market today. Corporate attorney James Gamble wrote in 2019 that many of our business leaders are compelled "to act like sociopaths,"[2] running their company as "a textbook case of antisocial personality disorder" in which it "is obligated to care only about itself and to define what is good as what makes it more money."[3] That same year, Marc Benioff, CEO of Salesforce, asked his "fellow business leaders" to wake up to the reality that "capitalism, as we know it . . . with its obsession on maximizing profits for shareholders . . . is dead."[4] Economist and Nobel Laureate Joseph Stiglitz warned that the way we practice business today is "exploitive" and that "the neoliberal fantasy that unfettered markets will deliver prosperity to everyone should be put to rest. . . . The rampant dishonesty we've seen from Wells Fargo and Volkswagen or from members of the Sackler family as they promoted drugs they knew were addictive—this is what is to be expected in a society that lauds the pursuit of profits as leading, to quote Adam Smith, 'as if by an invisible hand,' to the well-being of society, with no regard to whether those profits derive from exploitation or wealth creation."[5]

These criticisms could also be directed at the education system that helps shape and reward our business leaders, and in recent years there has been a wave of opinion pieces and books that are doing just that—many written by former students themselves. "Elite business schooling is tailored to promote two types of solutions to the big problems that arise in society: either greater innovation or freer markets," MIT Sloan School MBA student John Benjamin wrote in a searing 2018 *New Republic* article, adding "Proposals other than what's essentially *more business* are brushed aside."[6] In a 2019 *American Affairs* essay, Harvard Business School graduate Sam Long described an educational system that produces "a business elite dominated by financiers and their squires, presiding over a disordered economy gutted of both its productive energy and the ability to generate mass prosperity."[7]

Business journalist and writer Duff McDonald excoriated the business school environment in 2018, writing that the business curriculum is devoid of normative viewpoints, "has always cared less about moral leadership than career advancement and financial performance" and as a result, creates "a generation of corporate monsters" who lack "a functioning moral compass."[8] Also in 2018, Martin Parker, professor at the University of Leicester School of Management, charged that "we should call in the bulldozers and demand an entirely new way of thinking about management, business and markets."[9]

These critiques come at a time when capitalism is in crisis. One symptom of that crisis is income inequality, which is growing to epidemic proportions not seen since 1929. In 2016, the United States attained a Gini index, a measure of an economy's equality, of 41.5 (up from 34.6 in 1979), which ranks it as more unequal than India, Kenya, Russia, and the Philippines. This is a social crisis that capitalism both caused and seems unable to address. A second symptom lies in our natural environment, as global greenhouse gases are at their highest-ever level and show no signs of declining. The resulting climate change, coupled with the unrelenting destruction of natural ecosystems, led the United Nations to estimate that more than a million species are at risk of extinction. In fact, the human impact on the natural environment has reached such a level that scientists have proposed that we are now entering the Anthropocene; a new geological epoch in which we cannot describe the environment without including the role that humans are playing in influencing how it operates.

Growing segments of the population blame business leaders and other global power brokers for causing these problems. "We are in the beginning of a mass extinction. And all you can talk about is money and fairytales of eternal economic growth," sixteen-year-old Swedish climate change activist Greta Thunberg accused world leaders and executives at the United Nations Climate Action Summit in September 2019. Few were sympathetic to those executives, as polling from the Pew Research Center finds that large majorities of Americans believe our economic system unfairly favors powerful interests.[10]

## THE MARKET AS A NECESSARY SOLUTION

While I understand where feelings of distrust in the economic system are coming from, I don't think it's completely productive to heap all the blame for our era's crises on business and the market, looking for someone else to fix it. We are all complicit in the consumption and growth patterns that are feeding the social and environmental problems of our day, and many of us work in the very businesses we blame. We are facing systemic problems that require systemic solutions, and the pragmatic reality is that we must turn to, and work with, the market to solve these challenges. The market—comprising corporations, the government, and nongovernmental organizations, as well as the many stakeholders in market transactions, such as consumers, suppliers, buyers, insurance companies, banks, and so on—is the most powerful organizing institution on earth, and business is the most powerful entity within it. Though government is an important and vital arbiter of the market, it is business that transcends national boundaries, possessing resources that exceed those of many nations. Business is responsible for producing the buildings that we live and work in, the food we eat, the clothes we wear, the automobiles we drive, the forms of mobility we employ, and the energy that propels them. Indeed, if there are no solutions coming from business, there will be no solutions.

Business, for example, is developing the next generation of renewable energy, driving the average installed cost of wind power from 7 cents per kWh in 2009 to below 2 cents in 2019; wind power contributed 6.5 percent of the nation's electricity supply in 2019 (providing more than 10 percent in fourteen states and more than 30 percent in three states: Kansas, Iowa, and Oklahoma).[11] Similarly, innovations in solar photovoltaic power have led to a dramatic 99 percent decrease in price between 1980 and 2012,[12] leading to projections that solar power could climb from 7 percent of total US renewable generation in 2015 to above 35 percent by 2050.[13]

These examples do not mean that only business can generate solutions. Government policies can spur the market, and individual choices can feed it. But with its extraordinary powers of ideation, production, and distribution, business is best positioned to bring the change we need at the scale at which we need it. Without business, solutions will remain elusive. And without leaders who are willing to challenge taken-for-granted norms and conceive of a new vision for the corporation, such as Rose Marcario at Patagonia or Paul Polman at Unilever, business will never even try to find them. In fact, a 2017 survey by the Global Strategy Group found that 81 percent of Americans want businesses to "take action to address important issues facing society."[14]

But it's also apparent to me that those solutions will not be as visionary, transformative, or rapid as our world requires unless we change the business culture that produces them. To do that we must seriously rethink what students learn in business school. While business schools have made small and halting attempts over the years to address the misalignment between society's interests and those of business, they have not been enough. For example, two standard answers are to teach business students about ethics or the legal implications of corporate wrongdoing. But the first often strives to instill new values on fully formed adults or teach ethical reasoning to students who are paying a lot of money to learn other topics. The second only sets a worst-case baseline and does not inspire future business leaders to be their best, to achieve great things for their companies and for society. Both are isolated electives in an overall curriculum that teaches shareholder primacy above all else. Another answer is to ask graduating business students to sign an MBA oath at graduation time—a sort of management Hippocratic Oath to do no harm—that commits them to "create value responsibly and ethically" for the greater good.[15] While a nice idea, this oath comes late in the education process and with little preparation for what such an oath means. In truth, it often means little more than virtue signaling with no real accountability.

It is my belief that the prevailing business curriculum and its underlying philosophy need a profound overhaul. Our schools must teach students about the basics of business management. But they must also teach them to seriously consider the vast power that they may someday possess to shape and guide our society, and learn the responsibility to wield that power carefully. Tomorrow's business leaders should be taught to do something that previous generations rarely did: they must start thinking critically about the role of business in society, their role as a manager in guiding those businesses, and the overall system in which they will practice their craft—capitalism. They should be taught to look deep inside themselves to consider *management as a calling*—one that moves away from the simple pursuit of a career for private personal gain and toward a *vocation* that is based on a higher and more internally derived set of values about leading commerce and serving society.[16] It is about connecting your career with your conscience. As James Gamble writes, "power needs to be constrained by conscience."[17]

The process of developing that conscience and exploring one's calling cannot be accomplished simply by adding electives to the program. It requires a new approach to the curriculum, one that begins with a process of discernment by which students are both charged with a system of aspirational principles and encouraged to explore their own. Unfortunately, today's business education allows no such reflection. Classes, clubs, social activities, and the hunt for the first summer internship dominate their attention from the moment they arrive on campus.

The pursuit of a calling leads to the careful cultivation of wisdom, something lacking in today's business education. Business schools teach knowledge. This is what fills our research journals, and it is driven by theory and analysis that helps us first turn data into information and then turn that information into knowledge. The first step takes data in the form of artifacts, symbols, and information and examines relations for creating categories of information for analysis. The second step takes that information and examines patterns that allow us to develop useful "know-how" (see Figure 1).[18] But to turn that knowledge into wisdom requires one more step of an appreciation for principles.

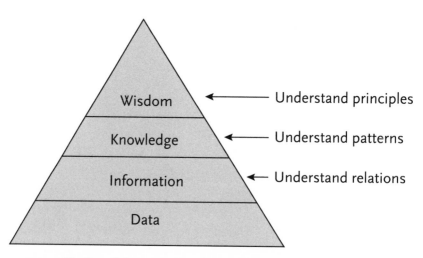

FIGURE 1    The Data, Information, Knowledge, Wisdom Pyramid.

The truth is that wise business leaders do not make decisions based solely on patterned information, regression analyses, and $p$-values. Instead, she or he assesses that knowledge and makes a decision based on wisdom, character, judgment, and integrity. Many of the problems we face in today's world are caused by applying knowledge without wisdom; "we act but we do not act wisely."[19] Developing the whole student, cultivating wisdom and character, requires a set of aspirational principles that guide the business education: how it selects and socializes its students; structures the curriculum, co-curriculum, and pedagogy by which they are molded; invites recruiters for placing them in positions of leadership; chooses the role models to elevate as exemplars of the principles they seek to reproduce; accepts donations that often leave a physical and cultural imprint on their facilities; and guides the research and rewards of its faculty.

Guided discernment, as part of that education, would counter the herd mentality that the pressures of business education create, leading to more focused, balanced, and mature students who will be thoughtful about why they are pursuing this education and how they might choose to direct it toward a career that is personally, professionally, and socially meaningful. Students need to be taught to become pillars of commerce that serve their shareholders, employees, and society, in a spirit of service similar to which we use to train doctors and lawyers. It is about embracing a revitalized set of professional and moral ideals. It's about developing conscience and character. And I would add an important addendum: if business schools do not provide this training in any formal way, students should take the initiative to add that content themselves. Today, many are doing just that by demanding more course content on sustainability and social impact.[20] But there must be more.

## THE DEMANDS AND TENSIONS OF A NEW
## GENERATION OF BUSINESS LEADERS

Twenty years ago, students who wanted to change the world turned to schools of public policy and nonprofit management for their training. Today, many are turning to schools of business management, and they are bringing with them a desire to explore a new sense of the economic, social, and environmental purpose of the corporation and their role as leaders. One survey found that 67 percent of business students want to incorporate environmental sustainability considerations into whatever job they choose;[21] another found that 88 percent of business school students think that learning about social and environmental issues in business is a priority and 83 percent state they are willing to take a salary cut for a job that makes a social or environmental difference in the world.[22] By 2019, business ethics had entered the top five most popular subjects for the first time, with nearly 25 percent of incoming students wanting a job focused on social impact after graduating and nearly 50 percent wanting to do so later in their careers.[23] Whereas previous generations of business students were exposed primarily to the idea that business should only be concerned with increasing profits for the shareholder (articulated most famously by Milton Friedman from the University of Chicago and Gordon Gekko in the movie *Wall Street*), many of today's business students show an interest in moving beyond such a narrow view and dedicating their careers to making a difference in the world.[24]

But business programs are not keeping pace with this reality. In his *New Republic* critique, MBA student John Benjamin argued that the curriculum stifles discussion of the common good while emphasizing the overriding objective of profit maximization as unquestioned. Rather than cultivating open-minded stewards of the economy, he argued, it teaches students to ignore shareholder capitalism's obvious ethical lapses and avoid any kind of systemic analyses of it.[25] Indeed, many students seem to graduate with a narrower understanding of business than when they entered the program. According to Craig Smith, professor of ethics and social responsibility at INSEAD, "Students come in with a more rounded view of what managers are supposed to do but when they go out, they think it's all about maximizing shareholder value."[26]

I watch my students struggle with these pressures. Many start their business education with aspirations to eschew big salaries and work to pursue social good no matter the income. And then they are immersed in a curriculum that walks them through a standard set of courses on economics, strategy, accounting, finance, operations, marketing, and organizational behavior, each built on a common underlying set of values that elevates profits, efficiency, and growth as unquestioned goods. One student told me that she felt that her values were under attack every time she walked into the building. This overriding culture and value set steers many into jobs they may not really want. William Deresiewicz lamented in his 2014 book *Excellent Sheep* that too many students are being shepherded toward jobs in consulting or finance because the worth of a college education is increasingly measured by "return on investment," with "return" measured as some "vaguely understood objectives: status, wealth— 'success,'" which usually translate into money.[27]

When students approach graduation, they look at the salaries that large consulting firms are offering peers and begin to bend from their former ideals. For some, it is the simple cultural cue that money signals status and success. For others, the process is much more pragmatic. In 2019, the median starting salary for an MBA graduate was $110,000,[28] while the top consulting firms offered an average of $165,000 per year with a starting bonus of $65,000.[29] This enticement can be too much to turn down, and some have little choice. College simply costs too much money, and they amass such large debt loads that they feel trapped. In 2019, a *Bloomberg* survey found that almost half of students at leading business schools borrowed at least $100,000 to finance their two-year degree.[30] And that creates a strange irony; we teach students how to become entrepreneurs and then saddle them with so much debt that they cannot afford to be entrepreneurs. In fact, research has shown that as student debt increases, the likelihood that a student will embark on a career in entrepreneurship declines.[31] To deal with the debt crisis, some accept high-paying jobs with the promise that they will leave once their student loans are paid off. But all too often, their cost of living soon includes homes, cars, vacations, retirement accounts, health care, and their own children's ballooning college costs, creating chains that hold them back from keeping that promise.[32]

Many will not even know that they have drifted from their previously noble goals, moving into gated communities behind protected walls, isolating themselves from the problems for which they begin to see no responsibility. They simply follow where they are led, neglecting the failures in the system that is rewarding them individually by damaging society as a whole. I remember once telling a successful investment manager that I wrote about ways in which the market can shift to address our sustainability challenges, and he dismissively replied that he didn't care about changing the market, adding, "I just want to know what the rules are, and beat the next guy [sic] at them." Martin Parker warned, "If we teach that there is nothing else below the bottom line, then ideas about sustainability, diversity, responsibility and so on become mere decoration."[33]

### TRAINING FUTURE BUSINESS LEADERS IN A VOCATION

The business curriculum should be restructured to emphasize that there is much more to business than the bottom line. And to do that, we should be encouraging students to look deep inside themselves, to discern what kind of business leader they wish to be and where to be it. We should ask them to consider more than their own personal success and consider how they can also serve society. Rather than only asking, "How much money will I make?" one may also ask, "What kind of legacy do I want to leave?" Instead of only asking, "What career track gives me the most opportunity for professional development?" one may also ask, "What pursuits will bring me closer to making a meaningful contribution to others in my business, my community, and society?" These are the kinds of questions that make a life worth living.

But it is only possible to discuss these kinds of questions if students are taught to examine critically the system that they are entering and potentially leading. These future business leaders need to be more critical about capitalism, both as it exists and as it should exist. This proposition is much less radical than it may initially sound, and students would do well to disregard the canard that questioning capitalism is the pursuit of a communist or socialist agenda (and all the political baggage that gets heaped onto those two words). While most business education takes the form and function of capitalism as a given, capitalism is actually quite dynamic and ever-changing to suit the evolving needs of society. As Fox News commentator Tucker Carlson pointed out, capitalism is "a tool, like a staple gun or a toaster. You'd be a fool to worship it. Our system was created by human beings for the benefit of human beings. We do not exist to serve markets. Just the opposite. Any economic system that weakens or destroys families is not worth having. A system like that is the enemy of a healthy society."[34]

Capitalism is not static, nor is it naturally derived like some law of nature. Through the nineteenth and twentieth centuries, new rules were established to block monopoly power, collusion, and price-fixing. In the future, new rules will again be established to address our twenty-first-century challenges of reducing (or even eliminating) greenhouse gas emissions, creating more equitable income scales including equal pay for women, or political lobbying for the public good and not just individual gain.

This may lead to accepted notions of capitalism taking some forms found in the many variants that exist—Japanese, American, and Scandinavian capitalism are very different on issues such as the role of government, collaboration, or the responsibilities of companies. Nordic capitalism, for example, provides taxpayer-funded free education and free health care—an idea that is quite divisive in America—as well as generous, guaranteed pension payments for retirees. Norway has a law requiring that 40 percent of board members at large firms be female. Japanese capitalism encourages strong linkages between government and business and between suppliers and customers (called Keiretsu) that many within the United States find puzzling or collusive. Future business leaders must be taught about these kinds of variants as well as the history of capitalism(s), the underlying models on which they are based,[35] and the ways in which they both serve and harm society if they are to assume any kind of role in shaping necessary improvements.

This review of capitalism will naturally lead to more critical thinking on the purpose of the corporation in society. Most business students will parrot that it is simply to "make money for its shareholders," even to the point of believing that US corporate law demands it, even though no such law exists. This notion emerged in the 1970s with the Chicago School of Economics and is not only inaccurate, but can also lead to market problems such as excessively short time horizons for investment planning and measures of success, and a focus on only one type of shareholder who, in the words of Cornell law professor Lynn Stout, is "shortsighted, opportunistic, willing to impose external costs, and indifferent to ethics and others' welfare."[36] These types of investors are one of the factors that helped spur the Great Recession of 2008. Even a historic acolyte of shareholder value like former GE CEO Jack Welch had turned against it, calling it "the dumbest idea in the world" and adding that "shareholder value is a result, not a strategy. . . . Your main constituencies are your employees, your customers, and your products."[37]

Business professor and management consultant Peter Drucker took a broader view than that, arguing in the 1950s that "the purpose of a company is to create a customer." Profits are one metric of how well the company performs this purpose, but ultimately, he argued, "the business enterprise . . . exists for the sake of the contribution which it makes to the welfare of society as a whole."[38] Such a notion leads to a completely different approach to the role and education of the corporate leader. It moves beyond a belief that human motivation and purpose are driven primarily by greed and avarice. A leader with a calling will think and act in ways that are not solely about shareholder wealth maximization. He or she will focus on influencing the overall market in which business operates, seeking solutions to economic, social, and environmental problems that are systemic in nature and bring together the broad array of market constituents to solve them.

This refocusing on systemic solutions within the market and the reexamination of the purpose of the corporation in creating them is the focus of Part 1 of this book. It centers on two main issues. First, the natural environment is undergoing unprecedented and rapid changes in response to human activity, and it is the market that is creating them: changing the global atmosphere, restricting the availability of clean water, warming and acidifying the world's oceans, and causing species to go extinct. Second, our society is growing more economically unequal, and it is again the market that is making it this way. Importantly, these each represent systemic problems that are interlinked with so much more. Barack Obama argued that "it is hard to figure out how to solve sustainability issues and climate change if you also have huge gaps in wealth and opportunity and education . . . as wealth becomes more concentrated and more and more energy is used up by the few, the many become resentful . . . it is hard for us, then, to mobilize . . . around taking collective action."[39] An article in the *Journal of the American Medical Association* linked income inequality to the three-year decrease in American life expectancy between 2016 and 2019.[40] While suicide and opioid addiction are the direct cause of the decline, the study concluded that it is economic insecurity and despair that is the underlying cause. And Joseph Stiglitz warned that our systemic problems feed on each other in a vicious cycle: "Greater economic inequality is leading, in our money-driven political system, to more political inequality, with weaker rules and deregulation causing still more economic inequality."[41] The increasingly perilous economic situation that many faced in the COVID-19 crisis illustrated this dynamic.

Yet business students are offered very little education on the mechanisms through which business activities affect the natural and social environments through resource extraction, supply chains, manufacturing, consumption, tax strategies, and political lobbying. Instead, they must be provided with some degree of natural and social scientific literacy to responsibly manage their companies. This literacy should reflect the latest science that is coming out of a diverse array of departments that lie within steps of the business school—public policy, sociology, political science, atmospheric sciences, environmental studies, and more. The business school curriculum must be broadened to include knowledge necessary to assume the responsibilities that come with the power that business leaders possess.

One area of power that rises above all others is the extent to which the corporate sector influences government policy, the focus of Part 2. It is surprising to me how few business schools offer courses on government lobbying, much less collaborative and constructive lobbying. Indeed, common perceptions are that government has no place in the market, that regulation is an unwarranted intrusion in the market, and that all lobbying is corrupt. These views are naïve and destructive. Government is the domain in which the rules of the market are set and enforced, and lobbying is basic to democratic politics as governments seek guidance on how to set the rules of the market and usher reforms as needed. Companies with a mindset focused on serving society can participate constructively in policy formation, seeking policies that help to make society and the economy strong and fair in the aggregate, not just for the select and affluent few.

For example, Intel was instrumental in calling attention to the horrors of conflict minerals in the Democratic Republic of Congo and lobbied to create provisions in the Dodd-Frank Act that require the tracking and disclosure of such mineral sourcing within the broader electronics industry.[42] Companies also worked with national governments to phase out ozone-depleting chemicals with the Montreal Protocol in 1987 and with the US government to set new efficiency standards on trucks in 2016. The 2015 Paris Agreement on climate change was helped greatly by the support of powerful business interests,[43] and many have since spoken out against President Trump's decision to withdraw from the treaty.[44] In each of these examples, business took a responsible position in bringing about a shift in the market through policy. But business students, even in the nation's top schools, are not learning how to do this kind of collaborative work with governments.

### WHAT'S RADICAL NOW BECOMES COMMON SENSE LATER

In some ways these proposed changes take me back to when I began my PhD in 1991; a joint degree in management and environmental engineering at MIT studying the evolution of corporate approaches to environmental issues. At that time, business schools did not recognize environmental and social issues as legitimate topics to be studied or taught. Many were puzzled when I asked them to serve as an adviser on my dissertation committee, asking why I was at a business school and not knocking on doors at a public policy school. The first business course I ever took that even remotely touched on these topics was offered at the Harvard Business School in 1992 and was called "Capitalism Constrained," treating environmental issues as a restriction on the economy. Those pushing for business and business education to take responsibility to society and the environment, such as Thomas Gladwin from New York University and Nigel Roome from Tilburg University, were more aggressive and confrontational, arguing for deep systemic changes in the market. And they were marginalized as external critics or subjective advocates.

Today the idea of deep systemic changes in the market and the call on business to pursue social and environmental good in addition to the bottom line is mainstream. In 2019, two hundred chief executives from the Business Roundtable, including the leaders of Apple, American Airlines, Accenture, AT&T, Bank of America, Boeing, and BlackRock, issued a statement that redefined "the purpose of a corporation" as investing in employees, delivering value to customers and dealing fairly and ethically with suppliers, and not just advancing the interests of shareholders.[45] In 2020, the World Economic Forum published a "manifesto" after its annual Davos conference that redefined "the universal purpose of a company" as one that "serves society at large . . . supports communities . . . pays its fair share of taxes . . . acts as a steward of the environmental and material universe for future generations."[46] In a survey by Accenture, nearly all (99 percent) of the CEOs of the world's largest companies said that sustainability issues are important to the future success of their businesses.[47] A 2019 survey of insurance industry executives ranked climate change as the top concern in the industry.[48] And a 2019 meeting of three secretaries of agriculture and the CEOs of major food companies discussed how to pivot American agriculture to address climate change.[49] These kinds of shifts in corporate priorities are finding a receptive audience in the next generation of business leaders.

To fill the demand of this next generation, business schools are starting to respond. From 2001 until 2011, the percentage of business schools that required students to take a course dedicated to business and society increased from 34 percent to 79 percent,[50] and specific academic programs on the topic can be found at many US MBA programs.[51] The Aspen Institute's "Ideas Worth Teaching" awards call out exemplars of this next phase of management education,[52] with course titles such as "Reimagining Capitalism" at the Harvard Business School; "Economic Inequality" at Virginia's Darden School of Business; "Alternative Economic Models" at the Audencia Business School; and "The End of Globalization" at Yale's School of Management.

As these courses exemplify, students embarking on a career in management today live in interesting times. They are coming into this field when the idea of business addressing environmental and social problems is becoming more accepted, and that's exciting. Businesses are publishing sustainability reports, talking about living wages and health care, creating positions for Chief Sustainability Officers, marketing sustainable hotels, selling sustainable food, and building sustainable cars. You can go into a company now and talk about its responsibility to society and executives are not going to look at you like you have three heads—like they did to me back in the early 1990s.

Yet this is not sufficient on its own to fix the massive challenges we face. It's great that Lawrence Fink, the CEO of BlackRock, the world's largest asset manager, sent a letter to CEOs of public companies in 2019 telling them that they have a responsibility not only to deliver profits but also to make "a positive contribution to society."[53] Yet BlackRock continues to invest in, and profit from, some of the most environmentally damaging companies on the planet.[54]

Systemic threats like climate change and economic inequality are meanwhile getting worse and more destabilizing, to the point at which organizations such as the World Economic Forum name them as top threats to the global economy. These problems create a whole new set of challenges for those who care about business management. Our economy is now threatening our way of life, both environmentally and socially, in ways that are unprecedented. And, as the stuttered response to the COVID-19 crisis revealed, we are unprepared to deal with it. There is a wonderful line by Stephen Jay Gould from Harvard, who wrote, "[W]e have become, by the power of a glorious evolutionary accident called intelligence, the stewards of life's continuity on earth. We have not asked for that role, but we cannot abjure it. We may not be suited to it, but here we are."[55] There is the challenge that business leaders face.

In conceptualizing this challenge, future business leaders must develop sound skills as change agents, understanding both change within the organization and changes outside that will drive it; this is the topic of Part 3 of this book. One way to drive change is by dealing with sustainability challenges as mainstream business issues and fitting them into the market as it exists. That is the way it has been addressed since I began my career as a business school professor in the mid-1990s. It is a mode of calling out the win-win scenario and the "it pays to be green" hypothesis first made prominent by Harvard business professor Michael Porter in the 1990s.[56] This messaging is acceptable, as it fits with what it means to be a business manager today and does not challenge the underlying models of the market. But it is incremental in its focus.

While this approach may slow the velocity at which we are approaching environmental and social calamity, it does not reverse course, as it does not get to the root of the problems. Many are beginning to call out the fallacy of the win-win scenario, arguing that tough choices have to be made in changing our economic system if we are to really address our problems. Anand Giridharadas, in his provocatively titled 2018 book *Winners Take All: The Elite Charade of Changing the World*, has argued that there are no easy win-win solutions and the systemic changes that are needed will not be embraced by the "thought-leaders" and "plutocrats" that he derides if such changes challenge the status quo that maintains their ability to amass wealth. "The entrepreneurs were willing to participate in making the world better," he wrote, "if you pursued that goal in a way that exonerated and celebrated and depended upon them."[57]

Such critiques lead to a second way to drive change. It is to be provocative, to push people and institutions out of their comfort zones and create transformational change at the systemic level. This is the realm of creative destruction, changing markets, and challenging taken-for-granted metrics such as gross domestic product and discount rates. Unilever, for example, ended the practice of issuing quarterly reports in 2018 to help managers think more about the long-term health of the company rather than short-term profits.[58] In 2019, Norway's $1 trillion sovereign wealth fund announced that it would divest from oil and gas exploration.[59] That same year, the European Investment Bank decided to end funding for fossil-fuel energy projects to support Europe's plan to become the first climate-neutral continent.[60] These announcements follow the ironic decision by the Rockefeller Brothers Fund in 2014, heir to Standard Oil tycoon John D. Rockefeller, to divest from fossil-fuel investments.[61] Such moves are provocative, as they create change at the system level. Therefore, they face resistance from those who benefit from the system as presently structured.

Blending the incremental and transformative ways of driving change, students of business management entering the market today have to be prepared to challenge the status quo and make people uncomfortable, while at the same time knowing when to be polite and fit our social and environmental challenges within the mainstream of the status quo. They're going to have to do both and know when each is warranted. That requires a knowledge of how social movements both drive and can be driven by corporations.

And that poses a further challenge for us as both change agents and human beings, a challenge that is the focus of Part 4. How can we push for systemic change while recognizing that we are also part of that system that needs change? Think about it; we are people who care about climate change, water scarcity, and social equity. And yet, our lives are not really sustainable. I, for example, give talks on climate change and am a frequent flyer on Delta Airlines. I drive a car, I have a house, and I eat meat. I am paid a good salary and enjoy great health care while 40 percent of Americans are presently unable to pull together just $400 for an emergency,[62] 78 percent live paycheck to paycheck,[63] 44 percent earn about $18,000 per year,[64] and 42 percent have saved less than $10,000 for retirement.[65] The reality represented by these sobering statistics was laid bare by the COVID-19 pandemic as many faced unemployment, hunger, and eviction without government support. The lengths people might go to when in such desperate conditions should concern us all. But how do we balance our more comfortable lifestyles with their plight? How do we push others to recognize the need for systemic changes in the market without also recognizing the need for systemic changes in our own lives? We need to know how to address the burdens of dissonance, hypocrisy, and guilt in ourselves. We need to know how to strike the right balance of living our values without pretending we are not similarly part of the problem.

In the end, this is a challenge of a vocation as opposed to a single-minded pursuit of money and status—to blend your personal and professional lives. I am often asked, for example, "What difference does it make if I change my lifestyle to reduce my carbon footprint? I am not going to make an appreciable dent in carbon emissions or the problems we face in the world today." I think that if that's going to be your metric, then you will lose the will to continue. But if you want to live a life of authenticity, if you want to live a life according to your values, if you want to live a life of integrity, you will adopt behaviors that are consistent with your values and you will stick to them for the long term. And this, ultimately, is the kind of clear-headed moral thinking that today's business schools should be teaching.

### FIND YOUR CALLING IN MANAGEMENT

My hope in this book is to accelerate the process that business students should be undertaking and many are: to help them start the process of examining their purpose in the world. Though many of my examples will be centered on sustainability issues because that is what I study, the contents of this book are for every business student and the hope that they will find their true purpose. The truth is that we all have a purpose to what we do. It's just that some purposes are more thoughtfully arrived at, while others may be more externally imposed or blindly accepted. A theologian once told me that he can tell you what you worship by how you spend your time because a vocation is the active manifestation of what you value. In the words of writer and English professor David Foster Wallace, "in the day-to-day trenches of adult life, there is actually no such thing as atheism. There is no such thing as not worshipping. Everybody worships. The only choice we get is what to worship."[66] Similarly, columnist David Brooks warned, "[B]e watchful over what you love, because you become what you desire."[67] That desire, love, or activity is your life's work, and satisfaction will come from knowing who you are and what you are called to do.

This is not easy, and we are often discouraged from even trying to find our calling. A college education is increasingly valued simply for the skills it provides to earn a salary and then achieve happiness by purchasing the goods that salary affords. This thinking crowds out the desire to learn how to live a meaningful and productive life that fulfills you. Our commercial society has boiled the pursuit of happiness that Thomas Jefferson wrote about in the Declaration of Independence into something superficial and economically based, telling you that happiness derives from consuming more stuff. Its central message is that your value is measured by what you accumulate and what others see, rather than by what you believe. Contrary to many messages in our society, individuality is not measured by your outward appearance—clothes, tattoos, posture—it is measured by how you think. College degrees, fancy cars, big houses, and happy Facebook posts: these have all become ways of proving to people around you that you have worth. But they are projections, and often false.

I want to personally challenge every business student, every business executive, and every business school professor to think about the system in which students are beginning their careers and to push back when it is steering them away from their calling. Pushing back means questioning the world you are inheriting and taking ownership of it to make it better for others—the people who will live with the decisions you make and the next generation of business leaders who will inherit the world you leave them. I want to provoke you as students to set the goal of leaving the world better than you found it. To do that, you have to think now about the legacy you want to leave and begin to make it—this is the focus of Part 5.

The choices you make now will leave imprints on your career and on the world around you for decades to come. Choose wisely. I am reminded of an interview that Tim Hall, careers scholar at Boston University, conducted with a highly successful mid-forties senior executive. He reported that she was unhappy with what she thought was success and had an epiphany one day when she looked in the mirror and realized, "Oh my god, a twenty-year-old picked my career!" To avoid her fate, I want to encourage business students to make wise and far-reaching choices today, to strive for greatness, and to measure that greatness by how others benefit from what you do. Think to serve in business, not just to accumulate.

I am not exaggerating when I say that the future of our society and our planet depends on it.

# PART 1

# SHIFTING THE ROLE OF BUSINESS

CHAPTER 2

# THE CHANGING CONTEXT OF BUSINESS

THE IDEA OF BUSINESS moving beyond simple notions of corporate social responsibility (CSR) and addressing social and environmental problems as a strategic concern is relatively new, dating to the mid-1990s. Still today, when I tell people that I hold joint positions between a school of business and a school of environment, many express puzzlement at the link between the two. Even within the university system, many of us who straddle such departments describe being seen as "tree huggers" by our business school colleagues and "capitalist sell-outs" by our environment school colleagues. But those who occupy a space between two communities that have limited ties or understanding can see opportunities that those from either community cannot. In the mid-1990s, there were only a few of us straddling those communities. Today, there are far more and the numbers are growing. What was once "heresy" in business and business school education is now becoming "dogma."[1] I knew that was true when I heard the dean of the Ross School of Business say in 2014 that "sustainability is table stakes in management education today." And there is so much more to do. A survey of corporate executives by Accenture found that 72 percent identified education as one of the critical development issues for the future success of their business sustainability efforts.[2]

Indeed, there is a crying need for more management education in this area, as the business world is finding itself faced with sustainability challenges to a greater degree. As stated in Chapter 1, another survey by Accenture found that nearly all (99 percent) of the CEOs of the world's largest companies said that sustainability issues are important to the future success of their businesses.[3] This reality was echoed and articulated by the Business Roundtable,[4] Black Rock,[5] and the World Economic Forum[6] when they each issued statements that challenged the notion that a corporation's sole purpose is to make money for its shareholders and that instead it must deliver positive value to society, pay its fair share of taxes, and protect workers and the environment, as well as by the hundreds of corporations that have adopted the United Nations Sustainable Development Goals (SDGs) to improve their impact on society and the environment. And yet, for all this effort and activity, the problems are getting worse. "Rather than go where the puck is," Wayne Gretzky famously said, "go where the puck is going to be."

Business schools should be training their graduates on both where the puck is and where it is going. Where the puck currently is leads us to eco-efficiency, sustainable products, ESG reporting (environmental, social, and governance), and the litany of corporate programs that have been designed over the past two decades to integrate environmental and social issues into corporate strategy. Today, however, that is not enough. We are facing a whole new type of problem, as we are causing damage to the environment on a completely different scale and scope. The world today's managers grew up in is not the same as the world that the next generation is growing up in. Companies operating today must have a strategy for the Anthropocene—indeed in the Anthropocene, environmental strategy *is* business strategy.

## THE ANTHROPOCENE

Scientists have proposed that we have entered a new geologic epoch. We have left the Holocene—the current geological epoch that began after the last glacial period approximately 11,650 years ago—and entered the Anthropocene[7]—the Age of Humans—so named to acknowledge the catastrophic effects of the world's 7.5 billion people on the planet in the form of system breakdowns such as climate change, species extinction, and ocean acidification. This shift reflects a completely new and expanding type of environmental challenge. We, as a species, have grown to such numbers, and our technology has grown to such power, that we are altering the ecosystem on a planetary scale. For example, the 2003 UN Millennium Ecosystem Assessment concluded that "over the past 50 years, humans have changed ecosystems more rapidly and extensively than in any comparable period of time in human history."[8] Since that report was published, the rate of change has not diminished. Today, for example, scientists believe that climate change represents an existential threat to future generations. In 2018, the Intergovernmental Panel on Climate Change warned that if we don't come to terms with climate change by 2030, damage to the global climate will be irreversible.[9] Impacts could include reduced food production as regions of the Earth become too hot and dry to grow crops, elevated storm severity as weather becomes more variable and violent, increased spread of vector-borne diseases as pests begin to migrate with the shifting climate, and accelerated glacial melting leading to rising sea levels and storm surge.

But climate change represents just one marker of the Anthropocene; there are eight other "planetary boundaries" beyond which we should not go if we want to maintain a safe environment for life on Earth (see Figure 2). We've crossed four of them already. For climate change, scientists have set a boundary limit for atmospheric $CO_2$ at 350 ppm; we are now at 400 ppm and climbing. The second is species extinction or biosphere integrity: a boundary limit of twenty species per million per year has been set and we are presently over one hundred, leading to the assessment that we are in the midst of the "sixth mass extinction," where as much as half of all present species could be extinct by 2100. The third is nitrogen pollution (biogeochemical flows): scientists set a boundary limit for industrial and agricultural fixation of $N_2$ at 35 teragrams per year and we are presently at 121 (with phosphorous pollution growing right behind it). The fourth is deforestation or land system change: scientists set a boundary of 62 percent of forested land remaining undisturbed and we are presently at 75 percent. Scientists are monitoring another four: freshwater use, atmospheric particulates (aerosol loading), chemical pollution (novel entities), and ocean acidification. Given that population will keep growing—there will be nearly ten billion people by 2050—these problems will only get more severe. One is on the mend: stratospheric ozone depletion has been reversed after the Montreal Protocol on Substances that Deplete the Ozone Layer was enacted in 1987, leading to an expected recovery of the ozone layer near the middle of the twenty-first century.

"Global businesses, international co-operation and the striving for higher ideals, these are all possible because for millennia, on a global scale, nature has largely been predictable and stable," David Attenborough told business leaders at Davos in 2019. "Now in the space of one human lifetime, indeed in the space of *my* lifetime, all that has changed." The famed naturalist concluded, "The Holocene has ended. The Garden of Eden is no more."[10] What does this shift mean for society and, important for the audience of this book, business?

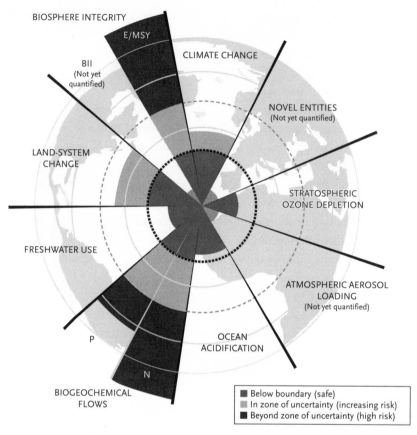

FIGURE 2   The Planetary Boundaries of the Anthropocene. Source: W. Steffen, K. Richardson, J. Rockström, S. E. Cornell, et.al., "Planetary boundaries: Guiding human development on a changing planet," *Science* 347 (2015): 736, 1259855, used with permission.

Business leaders will not be able to fully grasp these issues without a dose of natural science education in their training. It is the market that is changing the global atmosphere, restricting the availability of clean water, warming and acidifying the world's oceans, and causing species to go extinct. While rising population is certainly one driver of these shifts, the impact is compounded by the standard of living we all enjoy and the rightful desire of those in developing countries to enjoy a similar standard of living. Some have suggested that this new epoch should instead be called the "Capitalocene,"[11] as it is the market that provides the goods and services upon which these lifestyles are built and it is the market that encourages those lifestyles to be increasingly about consumption in the pursuit of profit and economic growth. In fact, much of these escalating impacts have been occurring since 1950 and the end of World War II, marking what scientists call the "great acceleration" during which environmental and social metric trajectories began to surge dramatically.[12]

But business students are offered very little education on the mechanisms through which business activities affect the natural environment. While there are courses that address resource acquisition, supply chain management, and manufacturing processes, students are taught how to optimize such activities by making them more efficient, with the over-riding goal of increasing corporate profits. Not enough attention is given to the extent to which these corporate activities are diminishing the integrity of the natural environment.

Instead, students should be provided with some degree of scientific literacy to responsibly manage their companies. For example, instead of planetary boundaries, Lancaster University business professor Gail Whiteman calls these the "key performance indicators" (KPIs) of the planet, and business leaders would do well to understand them and how they are changing them. In this way, we may begin to examine and alter notions of production and consumption that are setting society on a collision course with the ecosystem, seeking instead ways to disentangle profits or economic growth from material use or energy consumption. This takes business problem solving into a completely different domain than that of just offering green products. At the root, it is about challenging the belief that perpetual economic growth is either desirable or even possible, and instead examining ways to offer products and services that provide for human needs in ways that are not tied solely to the use and accumulation of material resources. Recognizing that mankind's "throughput"—the sheer weight of materials, including fuel, that feed the world's economies—increased by 800 percent in the twentieth century,[13] many have begun to reexamine ideas such as steady-state economies, or even economic "degrowth." In the words of economist and Nobel Laureate Robert Solow, the United States and Europe might soon find that "either continued growth will be too destructive to the environment and they are too dependent on scarce natural resources, or . . . they would rather use increasing productivity in the form of leisure."[14]

The costs of climate change to the US economy alone could reach hundreds of billions of dollars per year in lost labor productivity, declining crop yields, food shortages, early deaths, property damage, water shortages, air pollution, flooding, fires, and more. In 2020, a survey of global business leaders at Davos found that climate-related risks—extreme weather, failure to act on the climate, natural disasters, biodiversity loss, and man-made environmental disasters—were the top five concerns, the first time that has happened in the survey's fourteen-year history.[15] The Bank for International Settlements, an umbrella organization for the world's central banks, warned that same year that climate change could be one of the largest economic dislocations in history and "our community of central banks and supervisors cannot consider itself immune to the risks ahead of us."[16] With these sobering warnings as a guidepost, corporate executives can put their firm strategy into a longer arc—what the company and the world in which it will operate will look like in 2030, 2050, or 2100. These extended timelines are beyond most corporate planning horizons and could allow us to rethink some basic core assumptions about the purpose of the corporation, the objectives of the market, and the underlying models and metrics by which we evaluate those institutions.

Ultimately, this is the kind of transformative thinking we need to avoid collapse of the systems that support human life. Many companies are announcing pledges to go "carbon neutral" by eliminating $CO_2$ emissions from product operation, manufacturing, materials production, and energy sources.[17] How are they going to do it? They still don't know, but they do know that they won't find the answers if they don't begin asking really tough questions about the connection between material and profit, a focus on services not just products, new kinds of partnerships, and a renewed role for government in driving broad system change. And more extreme pledges by Microsoft[18] and Ikea[19] to go carbon negative will push the boundary of existing knowledge even further. Even entire countries (such as Iceland, Costa Rica, and New Zealand) have set goals to be carbon neutral by the middle of the twenty-first century. The mere question of carbon neutrality triggers a different level and kind of problem solving and puts us on a different path that compels a fresh look at what kind of world we will have in the next century. Right now, all we can say for sure is that systemic changes will transform the world in ways we cannot yet imagine. But new kinds of aggressive thinking today will yield new possibilities tomorrow.

For example, the auto sector is poised to be transformed in ways that will end personal car ownership, or dramatically diminish it, with exceptions in certain rural, farm, or other applications. Elon Musk sees the future of shared electric mobility as "obvious."[20] Even Bill Ford, great grandson of Henry Ford, warns that "cars can't continue to operate the way they have been, because we'll kill the world if China just cuts and pastes what we do."[21] This leads him to conclude that his company must implement business models that go beyond traditional car ownership.[22] There is a good chance that your children or grandchildren will never get a license or own a car; their conceptions of mobility will be fundamentally different. I can see this already in my classroom, as young people do not want the financial burden of a private automobile. A recent report predicted that the number of passenger vehicles on American roads could drop by 80 percent between 2020 and 2030, from 247 million to 44 million.[23]

Similarly, the energy sector will be fundamentally transformed such that the way our homes or offices get (and use) power will be fundamentally different. The US Department of Energy predicts that the future grid will use significantly more clean energy. But going further to the systemic level, it anticipates vastly more consumer participation and choice that will allow two-way flows of energy and information (including distributed generation, demand-side management, electrification of transportation, and energy efficiency) and holistically designed solutions (including regional diversity, AC-DC transmission and distribution solutions, microgrids, energy storage, and centralized-decentralized control).[24] The days of large baseload power plants and a centralized grid are coming to an end.

Within the food sector, the world's soon to be ten billion people will not be able eat as they do today. We will eat less meat and begin to think about alternative forms of protein, whether that's vegetarian or vegan lifestyles, plant-based meat substitutes, or insects such as crickets. That future is coming into view; for example, plant-based meat producer Beyond Meat had the most successful initial public offering (IPO) of 2019, with shares rising from $46 to $65.75 in its first day, giving the company a market value of nearly $3.8 billion.[25] Their product is now selling through fast food outlets like Burger King, as well as many major supermarket chains.[26] According to a report by Global Market Insights, the market for insects was about $33 million worldwide in 2015, but the US market alone could exceed $50 million by 2023.[27] Consulting firm A.T. Kearney predicted that by 2040 as much as 60 percent of the meat we eat will be either lab-grown or plant-based products that look and taste like meat.[28] Forward-thinking business leaders are preparing to either usher in these new realities or adapt to them.

But the systemic aspects of these changes are more than mere market shifts. The World Business Council for Sustainable Development, for example, is reexamining notions of consumption and considering what "sustainable consumption" might look like. Patagonia is exploring this question with its Common

Threads and Worn Wear initiatives, which encourage people to buy used clothing or repair damaged clothing in order to make it last.[29] Dell, Adidas, Method, and others have taken steps to address the critical issue of ocean plastics by developing programs to stop plastics from entering the environment, making new products with recycled ocean plastics, and developing alternatives to plastics such as biomaterials.[30] These are just a small number of early corporate actions that are part of an overall reexamination of the role of the market in the Anthropocene, the role of the corporation in that altered market, and the role of the executive in leading that corporation. They represent the next phase of business management.

# CHAPTER 3

# TRANSFORMING THE MARKET

THE MODERN ENVIRONMENTAL MOVEMENT that began in the 1970s and the corporate sustainability movement that began in the 1990s focused on discrete forms of pollution to our air, water, and land with such responses as pollution prevention, waste minimization, and eco-efficiency. Over time, attention grew to include toxic substances, hazardous waste, environmental justice, and other related environmental issues. In the late 1980s, the World Commission on Environment and Development (also known as the Brundtland Commission) added social concerns such as income inequality, living wages, secure retirement, and safe working conditions to round out the "triple bottom line" of the sustainability agenda: the 3 E's of environment, equity, and economy; or the 3 P's of people, planet, and profit.

Today, this "three-legged stool" of sustainability has become commonly accepted within business schools and business practice. Within business schools, what began as a modest offshoot of management science has grown into a maturing area of study. Within business practice, sustainability has entered most domains of corporate activity. Corporations print annual "sustainability reports," create positions such as the Chief Sustainability Officer, produce sustainable products (cars, hotels, food, and clothes), and gather for conferences on the "sustainability challenge." All of these efforts are geared toward the purpose of helping companies increase profits and using sustainability as a tool for doing that.

But in spite of the myriad new programs under the rubric of corporate sustainability, social and environmental problems continue to worsen and take new and systemic forms, such as stratospheric ozone depletion, climate change, water scarcity, ecosystem destruction, and species extinction. Sustainability activities have been integrated into corporate practice without serious changes in the core beliefs that underpin the root cause of these new types of problems, such that the resultant solutions do not actually solve the core problems. Sustainable business in its present form is reaching the limits of what it can accomplish. It is focused on incremental change, but it is not focusing on systemic change to set a new course away from our impending crisis. Instead of tinkering around the edges of the market with new products and services, business must now transform it. Let's consider two forms of business sustainability. The first is Enterprise Integration; the way we have been conceptualizing business sustainability since the mid-1990s. The second is Market Transformation, an emergent conceptualization that will be additive and eventually will replace the prior incarnation.[1]

### BUSINESS SUSTAINABILITY 1.0: ENTERPRISE INTEGRATION

The first phase of business sustainability, "enterprise integration," originated in the mid-1990s with the win-win scenario first made prominent by business professors such as Michael Porter[2] and business leaders such as Stephan Schmidheiny[3] and Chad Holliday.[4] It is founded on a model of business responding to market shifts to increase competitive positioning, and it does this by integrating sustainability into preexisting business considerations. This is not an appeal to morals or CSR but a response to key business constituents that are bringing sustainability to the corporate agenda through core business concerns. In the face of a market shift, companies must adapt and innovate—such as the shifts to low- or no-VOC paints (volatile organic compounds), to organic foods, to green cleaners, or to sustainable clothing. This exposes questions that early proponents of the win-win scenario asked, such as "Does it pay to be green?" as making little to no sense. It is the same as asking, "Does it pay to innovate?" The answer is not a simple yes or no because it depends on who does it, when they do it, and how they do it. It requires smart and strategic business thinking, and it is not easy.

Framing business sustainability as a market shift, the notion is that key external constituents bring the issue to business attention through existing functional departments, thereby making it a strategic concern. When insurance companies apply sustainability pressures, for instance, the issue becomes one of risk management. From competitors, it becomes an issue of strategic direction. From investors and banks, it becomes an issue of capital acquisition and cost of capital. From suppliers and buyers, it becomes an issue of supply chain logistics. From consumers, it becomes an issue of market demand.

Put in such terms, much of the specific language of sustainability recedes, being replaced by the core language of standard business strategy. Sustainability becomes less an external issue and more a core business issue as the firm's business channels bring it to managerial attention through preexisting avenues related to marketing, accounting, finance, operations, and so on. In each case, the firm has a preexisting model and language with which to conceptualize the issue and formulate a response. By realizing this "fit," firms can begin to see sustainability as a strategic issue, directed no longer by external concern but by internal strategic interests, as shown in Figure 3. For example, Clorox entered the green cleaner market in 2008 because it saw a potential to expand its product offerings and increase consumer demand and market growth; BP launched its (ill-fated) "Beyond Petroleum" campaign in 2000 as a way to improve its corporate reputation and attract more young recruits to join the company; and automobile companies are developing alternative drivetrains to respond to (or even get ahead of) regulatory requirements and expand their portfolio to appeal to a wider range of consumer interests. These are examples of corporate actions that address sustainability by striving to respond to mainstream business concerns.

The challenge for the business manager is to determine which frames work best in the particular organization. If you want to engage the strategic core of a consumer goods company like Proctor & Gamble, the key is to connect sustainability to consumer demand. Within a global retail company like Walmart, connect it to supply chain logistics and lowering the costs of moving products around the world. Within a manufacturing company like General Electric, connect it to operational efficiency and the ability to reduce the cost of production processes. For companies in the auto sector like Audi and Toyota, connect it to new product development, moving into hybrid and electric drivetrains and eventually driverless mobility, as these are the future of the sector.

Whirlpool is proud to point out that it never talks about climate change. Instead it talks about appliance energy efficiency, not because of corporate social responsibility, but because it has watched energy efficiency move from number

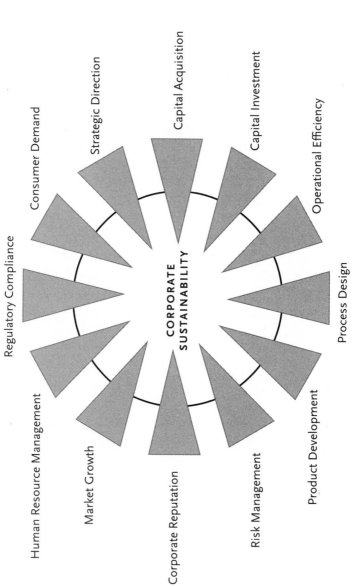

FIGURE 3  Multiple Frames for Communicating the Business Imperative of Sustainability. Source: A. Hoffman, *Competitive environmental strategy: A guide to the changing business landscape* (Washington, DC: Island Press, 2000), used with permission.

ten or twelve in consumer priorities in the 1980s to number three, behind cost and performance. And it expects those concerns will continue to grow as people become more cost-conscious about energy and water use. In the words of one executive, "We've got a train moving on efficiency. We'd just start confusing things if we tried to throw more on the train or start a new train."[5]

In this way, companies can remain agnostic about the science of particular issues (such as climate change) but still recognize their importance as business concerns. In doing so, they are turning the false dichotomy between the economy and the environment on its head. This is the first model of business sustainability, and it would seem to be setting us on a path to becoming more sustainable.

But not so fast. As promising as these developments are, our world continues to become less, not more, sustainable, and the types of problems we face are markedly different from what they were in the 1990s. The challenges of the Anthropocene have broad implications for how we think about business sustainability. Rather than fitting sustainability into the existing models of the market, we must now recognize that the market is taking control of natural systems with potentially catastrophic consequences. Markets are intrinsically growth-oriented and, in the words of Richard Reeves at *The Guardian*, "don't work well in a stationary state; they are like sharks, either moving or dead."[6] But perpetual growth is not possible and its continued pursuit is self-destructive,[7] as it leads to excessive consumption, resource use, and waste production. Climate change, ozone depletion, food insecurity, water scarcity, and the social unrest that results all point to a fundamental system failure created by our market (and political) institutions. I don't always agree with Naomi Klein when she says that we need to shred the free-market ideology and come up with a new system to address climate change, but I agree with her point that we struggle to find a way out of this crisis because doing so would "fundamentally conflict with deregulated capitalism" and that we have to "come face to face with the hard truth that the conveniences of modern consumer capitalism [are] steadily eroding the habitability of the planet."[8]

As a result, the first phase of business sustainability—integrating these practices within core corporate functions—is inadequate for the scope of the issues we now face. By framing sustainability strictly as a continuing shift in ordinary strategic concerns from existing stakeholder demands, the full scope of the issue cannot be realized. Responses will not be dictated by ecosystem constraints or social realities, but rather by internal and external strategic goals that yield routinized responses. These responses are generally grounded in strategies for eco-efficiency and profit maximization, which do not challenge the fundamental underlying models of business that are actually causing the problems in the first place: neoliberal notions of trade, the overriding imperative of efficiency as an unquestioned good, the Darwinian notion of markets as domains of conquest and domination, and others that form the crux of business education today. For the long term, corporate sustainability strategies must move beyond *reducing unsustainability* and move toward *creating sustainability*.[9] That shift requires a new model of thinking.

### BUSINESS SUSTAINABILITY 2.0: MARKET TRANSFORMATION

The next mode of business sustainability, "market transformation," involves corporations making systemic changes in the business environment instead of waiting for a market shift to create incentives for sustainable practices. We can see some of the elements of this shift coming into view along two initial categories: systemic corporate strategies and new ways of doing business.[10]

### Systemic Corporate Strategies

Real sustainability is a property of the system.[11] It cannot be measured by one company or one product but must include the entire system of which it is a part. The notion of an energy company installing a windfarm and calling itself sustainable makes no empirical sense. A more sustainable energy system incorporates the whole grid, encompassing generation, transmission, distribution, use, and mobility. Google, for example, plans to run all of its data centers entirely from renewable energy.[12] This goes far beyond a token commitment, creating a hedge against future energy volatility by changing the overall energy system on which the company depends to make it more stable and reliable while reducing its contributions to climate change. Other examples include Michelin's efforts to change the supply chain on rubber[13] or companies such as Perdue and Tyson striving to reduce or eliminate the use of antibiotics in chicken[14] and move into alternative protein markets.[15] These changes call for new conceptions of operations, partnerships, government engagement, and transparency.

For example, systemic corporate strategies involve the optimization of operations and supply-chain logistics to move away from linear production models in which raw materials are extracted, turned into products, sold to consumers, and disposed of at the end of their lives. Instead, new models are being used to reduce the need for raw materials and the creation of waste, such as life-cycle analysis, which examines the total environmental and economic costs of product from "cradle to grave"; industrial ecology, which seeks to link waste streams from one company that may be used as a feedstock in another; and the circular economy, which is a framework for reducing material and energy use among all the constituents in the supply chain by designing recyclability into initial designs and recycling in a way that keeps materials at their highest value (rather than, for example, merely burning them for fuel).

In the realm of strategy, it involves looking to novel partnerships with non-profits, government, competitors, and seemingly unrelated companies to create new types of business models. For example, the Ford Motor Company experimented with an unusual partnership between Whirlpool, Sunpower, Eaton, Infineon, KB Homes, and Georgia Tech in the MyEnergi Lifestyle initiative to envision how future American homes would be integrated and optimized in a holistic and efficient way. Home solar panels use the photons produced by sunlight to generate direct current (DC) electricity that is turned into alternating current (AC) before being fed into the home's wiring system. But your appliances, like computers, use a transformer to turn that AC power back to DC power. This is obviously wasteful, and the program examined the feasibility of an entirely DC home. This would require DC-powered appliances, such as dishwashers and dryers, that could then be further optimized by employing grid-monitoring technologies that inform your clothes washer to run or your refrigerator to go into the defrost cycle when demand is lowest (or in the event of real-time energy pricing, when energy is cheapest). All of these coordinated efforts would make the home and the grid more energy efficient at a systemic level and not just on an individual component basis.

To think more systemically, one step is to examine the metrics used for economic calculations which can lead to actions that worsen our sustainability problems. Economist Nicholas Stern stirred a healthy debate in 2007 when he questioned the use of discount rates when calculating the future costs and benefits of climate change mitigation and adaptation.[16] Using an unusually low rate of 1.4 percent, he argued that it is inherently unethical to use standard discount rates on certain issues. For example, most large multinational corporations use a discount rate between 5 percent and 10 percent in cash flow analyses. But a discount rate of 10 percent has the implicit assumption that anything ten years out and longer is worthless. Is that true? Arturo Cifuentes of Columbia University and David Espinoza from Geosyntec Consultants argue that valuation techniques like the discounted cash flow method are "anchored in arcane ideas" that "favor short term gains at the expense of future generations."[17] That is the future of your children and your grandchildren.

Many have begun to question that value and the accuracy of standard measures of national economic health. The COVID-19 crisis, for example, brought to light the disconnect between stock market indices, such as the Dow Jones Industrial Average, and the actual health of the economy. In the summer of 2020, the Dow Jones showed steady growth[18] while at the same time the economy posted its worst drop on record[19] and unemployment reached historic highs.[20]

Another metric of economic well-being, gross domestic product (GDP) has also come under scrutiny for its focus strictly only on the movement of money. The problem is that some monetary exchanges are desirable and others are not. I, for example, may choose to eat all my meals at Krispy Kreme Donuts and McDonalds, and GDP will go up. Then I have a heart attack and go to the hospital, and GDP goes up. Then I die and my family pays for a funeral and burial, and GDP goes up again. Are all these of equal value? Of course not. Does this kind of example play out in real life? Yes. The country of Madagascar sought to increase GDP by increasing its production and export of wood. But in the process, the country deforested at such an alarming rate that it hampered future cash flows from this renewable resource. The goal of GDP growth sent them in the wrong direction.[21] To find alternatives to GDP, Bhutan has instituted the Gross Happiness Index, and former French president Nicolas Sarkozy formed a commission (including two Nobel Laureates, Amartya Sen and Joseph Stiglitz) whose report recommended new metrics that shift economic emphasis from simply the production of goods to a broader measure of overall well-being that would include considerations for overcoming the ways in which GDP overlooks the value of wealth to be passed on to the next generation; economic inequality (with the result that most people can be worse off even though average income is increasing); and the environmental impacts of economic decisions.[22]

Other steps in thinking more systemically include using corporate marketing power to inform and educate the general public on decisions that lead to more sustainable outcomes; exploring new forms of governance models (such as ESOPs, COOPs, hybrid organizations, and B Corps) that can be used for different purposes; and implementing new forms of employee engagement that help employees thrive within the organization (such as Positive Organizational Scholarship[23] and Appreciative Inquiry[24]). B Corporations, such as Patagonia, set explicit standards for verified social and environmental performance, public transparency, and legal accountability to balance profit and purpose and build a more inclusive and sustainable economy. On a smaller scale, Argus Farm Stop in Ann Arbor is legally registered as a low-profit limited liability company (L3C) to create a model that earns an appropriate operating profit but focuses on providing fair profit margins to the local farmers that stock the shelves; where standard retail models pay farmers just 14.8 cents of profit on the dollar, Argus pays 75 cents.[25]

### New Ways of Doing Business

Market transformation also challenges traditional ways of conceiving of the market, including corporate purpose, consumption, and its underlying models. Market transformation calls for a reexamination of the purpose of the corporation as simply to make money for its shareholders. Anyone in business will tell you that the motivations of corporate executives and their resultant strategies are far more complex. It also forces us to examine new models of sustainable production and consumption, calling on businesses to, in the words of the World Business Council on Sustainable Development, "abandon the existing consumption paradigm" and move toward "transformations in mainstream lifestyles and consumption patterns."[26]

Market transformation calls for increased transparency to gain both internal management clarity and external validation, under the watchful eye of activists, investors, suppliers, buyers, employees, and customers. Consider the unusual actions of food giant Nestlé, which in 2015, after a year-long internal investigation, found forced and abused labor in its seafood supply chain from Thailand, disclosed the report's conclusions, and warned competitors that they too might be supporting human rights violations.[27] Mark Lagon, president of the nonprofit Freedom House, an anti-trafficking organization, called this decision "unusual and exemplary," because "the propensity of the PR and legal departments of companies is not to fess up, not to even say they are carefully looking into a problem for fear that they will get hit with lawsuits." Nestlé made public promises to impose new requirements on all suppliers, train boat owners and captains about human rights, hire outside auditors, and assign a high-level Nestlé manager to make sure that these efforts are effective.

Finally, market transformation requires compelling new business models to augment traditional ones that dominate business thinking, such as neoclassical economics and agency theory. Both of these models are built on rather dismal simplifications of human beings as largely untrustworthy and driven by avarice, greed, and short-term thinking. As these models are questioned, new

**1**

## ENTERPRISE INTEGRATION

- Level of analysis: Corporation/Product/Service
- Model: Translate into preexisting business considerations
- Objective: Reduce unsustainability
- Example: Reduce carbon emissions

- Will help students get a job in today's markets
- Foundational for business sustainability

**2**

## MARKET TRANSFORMATION

- Level of analysis: System
- Model: Transform markets by reexamining unchallenged assumptions
- Objective: Create sustainability
- Example: Go carbon neutral/negative

- Will help students set a vision for tomorrow's markets
- Additive to Enterprise Integration

TABLE 1  Business Sustainability: Two Views. Source: A. Hoffman, *Business sustainability as systems change: Market transformation,* Conceptual Note #5-720-388 (Ann Arbor, MI: WDI Publishing, 2019), used with permission.

ones are emerging, from regenerative capitalism to collaborative consumption, from conflict-free sourcing to the sharing economy. While these are just four models that have emerged as ways to reorient the economy, there are many more coming forward. The question is not which is right and which is wrong. Rather, they are all iterations and experiments leading to a shift in the overall models we use to understand how the market works in ways that attend to our broader challenges, and questioning what Elizabeth Kolbert warns is an economy that "is destroying the planet, the very basis of civilization, because there is profit in it."[28] Ultimately, this expansion of new business models will begin to coalesce around a composite model that brings the full scope of market transformation into greater clarity.

## UNDERSTANDING THE SHIFT THAT IS UNDER WAY

The market is shifting and business management is shifting with it. Business leaders must be trained to continue these shifts, and the two models shown in Table 1 offer a guide. The first phase of business sustainability, Enterprise Integration, is founded on a model of business responding to market shifts to increase competitive positioning by integrating sustainability into preexisting business considerations. By contrast, the second phase of business sustainability, Market Transformation, is founded on a model of business transforming the market through changes in the system around it.[29]

The first phase is geared toward the present-day measures of success; the second phase will help companies create tomorrow's measures. The first is focused on "reducing unsustainability"; the second is focused on "creating sustainability." The first is incremental, the second transformational. The first attends to symptoms; the second attends to causes. The first focuses primarily inward toward the health and vitality of the organization; the second expands that focus to include an outward look toward the health and vitality of the market and society in which the organization operates. The first will help future leaders get a job in today's marketplace; the second will help them develop a target for a lifelong career.

CHAPTER 4

# ADDRESSING CLIMATE CHANGE

ALTHOUGH THE ANTHROPOCENE poses many challenges and opportunities for business, climate change in particular deserves special focus. This is in part because the impacts of global temperature rise on the market can potentially be so massive as to hobble entire companies, sectors, or economies. And yet, assessing its impact is one of the great challenges of responding to the issue, both as a business and as a society. That's because the threat it poses can be so hard to see or feel. One cannot see greenhouse gas increases; one cannot feel global mean temperature rise. In the wake of Hurricanes Florence, Michael, or Dorian for example, one may be compelled to ask, "Was that climate change?" But even as science's abilities for attribution are getting better, businesses need more than scientific inference and general warnings to plan their activities with climate change in mind; they need hard financial data.[1]

I saw this first-hand in 2013, when I helped convene a series of executive forums to introduce a wide range of business executives to the 30 petabytes—30,000,000,000,000,000 bytes—of weather and climate data in the National Climatic Data Center's possession.[2] While the hope was that they would see the value of such vast amounts of data in managing climate risk, we found limited interest, leaving us to wonder if we were too early and whether our target was too broad.

This caused me and others to realize that we should be more focused on two specific sectors for bringing this data to the market. One is the field of management consulting, which seems to be stepping into the fray, selling personalized climate risk reports to corporations, a move that some fear will privatize climate data and exclude many from accessing it.[3]

The other sector is insurance, which can take this data and diffuse it widely through the economy. Insurance companies are society's first line of defense in absorbing the costs of climate change, making this industry arguably the one most directly affected by the issue. Insurers must measure the ever-changing global trends of climate change impacts and provide as much specific quantifiable detail as possible on the costly risks they impose. In this respect, insurers act as neutral brokers in communicating the reality and the dangers of climate change. They are looking at the numbers and have no political interest in this debate, reframing the issue in terms business people can understand. In the end, this kind of reframing is central to reaching the right audiences for change.

### REFRAMING CLIMATE CHANGE

Jane Lubchenco, an environmental scientist who oversaw the National Oceanic and Atmospheric Administration (NOAA) from 2009 to 2013, offered a clever analogy to explain the connection between the destruction wrought by a single hurricane and climate change. It involved steroids and baseball.

Her analogy goes like this. If a baseball player takes steroids, it's hard to connect one particular home run to his drug use. But if his total number of home runs and his batting average increases dramatically, the connection becomes apparent. "In similar fashion, what we are seeing on Earth today is weather on steroids," Lubchenco explained. "We are seeing more, longer lasting heat waves, more intense storms, more droughts and more floods. Those patterns are what we expect with climate change."[4] And those weather patterns come with a cost.

In 2017, for example, Hurricanes Harvey, Irma, and Maria and other natural disasters such as Mexican earthquakes and California wildfires caused economic losses of $330 billion (both insured and uninsured), making it the second costliest year in history for natural catastrophes with almost double the inflation-adjusted annual average of $170 billion over the prior ten years.[5] The total economic losses from wildfires alone in the US in 2017—the third-hottest year on record, behind 2016 and 2015[6]—were four times higher than the average of the preceding sixteen years, while losses from other severe storms were 60 percent higher.[7]

And the costs continue to mount. In 2018, the estimated costs from Hurricane Florence, which struck the Carolinas, were estimated at $14 billion, of which $5 billion were insured, making it the costliest hurricane that ever hit the United States.[8] The Camp Fire hit California that same year, killing eighty-six people and becoming the costliest wildfire in the state's history with $16.5 billion in damages, of which $12.5 billion were insured.[9]

These are the trends that have insurance companies watching very closely. Data from Munich Re show a steady increase in the frequency (see Figure 4) and costs (see Figure 5) of natural disasters between 1980 and 2018. In 2019, it became the first major insurer to explicitly link California's wildfires to climate change, issuing a white paper that warned, "Climate trends also show an increase in wildfire hazard, which is arguably higher now than it ever was in the 20th century. This illustrates that the overall risk and loss levels are significantly different than in the past. And as the state's climate continues to change, California will experience a further worsening of these conditions in the medium term."[10]

This projection has undeniable financial consequences for the insurance industry, which paid out a record $135 billion for natural catastrophes in 2017, almost three times higher than the annual average of $49 billion.[11] That's not to mention the $195 billion in uninsured losses that were also incurred. Uninsured losses from 2012's Hurricane Sandy were 50 percent of the total $65 billion in losses, a staggering tab picked up by individual citizens and the taxpayer.

At its most extreme, some worry whether either a single event or cluster of events could cripple global or national insurance sectors. Some speculate that a Category 5 hurricane hitting Miami would put the $3.7 trillion in Florida coastal properties in harm's way, causing insured losses that could reach between $150 billion and $250 billion. But even that number could be low for the worst-case scenario. The Centre for Risk Studies at Cambridge University's Judge Business School modeled a Category 4 hurricane hitting Florida Bay, slightly south of Miami, and then heading northwest to Tampa and Pensacola, in its wake causing total physical damage in excess of $1.35 trillion.[12]

As the insurance sector adjusts to factor these growing risks of climate change into coverage and premiums, it will change our economy with higher costs that will affect everyone's pocketbook and therefore everyone's ability to understand the risks we face from this existential crisis. This could address one of the great challenges of communicating climate change; how to make it personally salient. One of the best ways to make it salient is to put a dollar sign

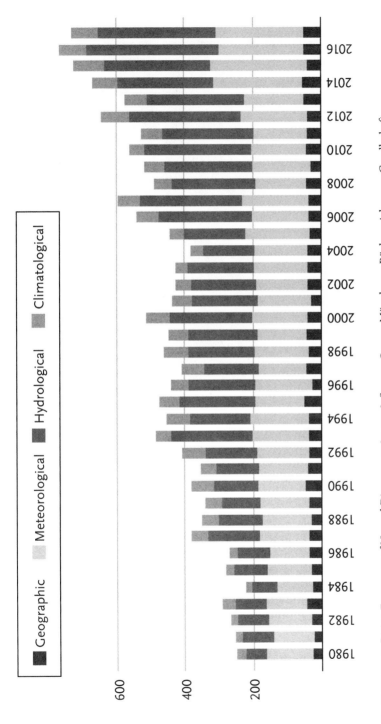

FIGURE 4 Rising Frequency of Natural Disasters, 1980–2018. Source: © 2020 Münchener RückversicherungsGesellschaft, NatCatSERVICE, used with permission.

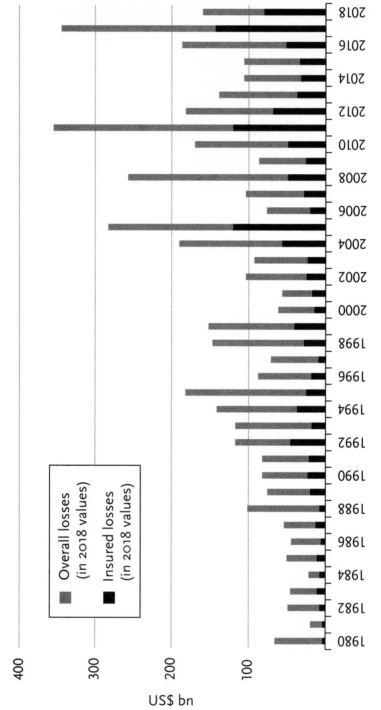

FIGURE 5 World Natural Catastrophes by Overall and Insured Losses, 1980–2018. Note: Inflation adjusted via country-specific consumer price index and consideration of exchange rate fluctuations between local currency and US$. Source: © 2020 Münchener RückversicherungsGesellschaft, NatCatSERVICE, used with permission.

on it, and insurance will do that. Our abilities to drive a car, buy a house, build an office building, run a manufacturing plant, and enter into contracts are all supported by insurance. Without it, a great deal of these activities would become more expensive or even stop. "If the risk from wildfires, flooding, storms or hail is increasing then the only sustainable option we have is to adjust our risk prices accordingly. In the long run it might become a social issue. . . . Affordability is so critical [because] some people on low and average incomes in some regions will no longer be able to buy insurance," Munich Re's chief climatologist Ernst Rauch warned in 2019.[13]

### A WHOLE NEW BALLGAME

While reinsurance companies such as Munich Re and Swiss Re, which insure the insurers, have been studying increasing climate-related risks for decades, traditional insurance companies with more familiar names like State Farm, Travelers, and Liberty Mutual have been slow to respond. There are two primary reasons for this. The first is that they've been able to pass on the most catastrophic or uncertain risks to reinsurers and other investors. The second is that insurers are overconfident that they'll be able to quickly adjust their policies on a year-to-year basis to manage climate risks.[14] Warren Buffett, for example, told shareholders in 2018 that "[n]o company comes close to Berkshire in being financially prepared for a $400 billion megacat [megacatastrophe]. Our share of such a loss might be $12 billion or so, an amount far below the annual earnings we expect from our non-insurance activities."[15] He was not alone. A 2012 study found that only 12 percent of insurance companies had a comprehensive climate change strategy.[16]

But this is changing. A 2018 study found that 38 percent of insurance companies considered climate change to be a core business issue,[17] and that same year, the International Association of Insurance Supervisors, a respected international standard-setting body for the insurance sector, published a report outlining climate risk as a strategic threat for that sector.[18] The report warned, "It is important to recognize that insurers may be well-versed in understanding the dynamics of such extreme events, and may be able to adjust exposures through annual contract re-pricing. However, the potential for physical climate risks may change in non-linear ways, such as a coincidence of previous un-correlated events, resulting in unexpectedly high claims burdens."

It would appear that many insurance underwriters began to listen. A 2019 survey by the Society of Actuaries found that 267 actuaries identified climate change as their top emerging risk. In fact, climate change was referred to as "the survey's big mover . . . in a dramatic shift from previous years . . . it is now considered the top current risk (12%), top emerging risk (22%), top combination risk (11%), and is second among top five emerging risks (49%, with a leading increase of 20%)."[19]

Recognizing this threat, many insurers threw out decades of outdated weather actuarial data and hired teams of in-house climatologists, computer scientists, and statisticians to redesign their risk models.[20] Ultimately, they began to examine whether they needed to change their coverage and raise their rates. In 2019, both the Liberty Mutual Group[21] and Chubb,[22] the largest commercial insurance company in the US, announced that they would stop insuring thermal coal plants. Goldman Sachs followed suit, announcing that it would no longer provide financing for projects that support either Arctic oil exploration and development or new coal-fired power generation unless it included carbon capture.[23] It is possible that the finance sector may be able to create a market shift that governments seem unwilling to do by passing a carbon price. And these moves to monetize the climate change issue will compel citizens, businesses, and governments to perk up and pay attention.

### AND YET IT CHANGES

When Galileo Galilei upset dominant beliefs in the sixteenth century by asserting that the Earth revolved around the sun and was forced to recant, he is purported to have replied, "Eppur si muove," meaning "and yet it moves." Today, although many dispute that the climate is changing, one might offer a similar retort: "And yet it changes."

As humans persist in the emission of greenhouse gases, the climate continues to change; weather patterns become more unstable; damages due to hurricanes, wildfires, droughts, and floods increase; and insurance payouts grow. In response, insurance premiums increase and coverage decreases (as many found after they tried to rebuild after the Camp Fire in California[24]). This leads to shifts in the market beyond renewable energy, alternative drivetrains, and increased efforts at carbon neutrality. It also leads to new building standards for resiliency, new behaviors that curb our carbon footprints, and ultimately a new awareness that sees increased storm severity for what it is: a consequence of climate change.

These will be major influences on business—*all* business—moving into the coming years and decades. As businesses take on the challenge, they will compel others within society to give it the seriousness it demands. And that includes business schools. Future business leaders must be trained for the "new normal," a world in which climate change takes hold within markets, altering financial calculations, supply chain reliability, resource availability, and other aspects that are central to the business curriculum and business practice.

# PART 2

# REBUILDING THE ROLE OF GOVERNMENT

CHAPTER 5

# RETHINKING
# BUSINESS-GOVERNMENT
# ENGAGEMENT

"We're in a hell of a mess in every direction. . . . Respect for
government, respect for the Supreme Court, respect
for the president, it's all gone."

**PAUL VOLCKER**, former Federal Reserve Chairman (1979–1987), made this statement in a 2018 op-ed for the *New York Times*, worrying that "I don't know, how you can run a democracy when nobody believes in the leadership of the country?"[1] Volcker had reason to worry. According to a 2017 Gallup poll, 81 percent of Americans disapproved of the way Congress was handling its job.[2] According to Frank Newport, reporting for Gallup News, "That's the lowest rating for any business or industry sector we tested," adding that "Americans think that Congress is corrupt and not focused on the interests of the people."[3] The Pew Research Center observed, "The public's trust in the federal government continues to be at historically low levels. Only 19 percent of Americans today say they can trust the government in Washington" and that this represents a steady decline from "1958, when the American National Election Study first asked this question, 73% said they could trust the government."[4]

This distrust affects how people view government's relationship to business. As I talk with business students, I see a vast number today who have a stated belief that government has no role to play within the market, and that regulation is generally a restraint and intrusion in the functioning of the market. This is cause for concern: for the market, for society, and for the students' individual careers. The truth is that the market requires government to function properly, providing rules by which commerce is to be conducted on such things as establishing property rights, enforcing contracts, insuring banks, establishing subsidies and tariffs, setting monetary and fiscal policy, establishing trade rules, protecting the natural environment, providing a social safety net for the less fortunate, and more. In fact, the US Constitution gives the government the power to regulate commerce. The truth is also that government needs business to provide information, data, knowledge, and research on which to set sound policy on many topics. And a lack of training for future business executives on either of these dimensions hampers their ability to properly understand the market, the policies that govern it, and their ability to lead their companies in that context.

But the attitude of today's business students toward government doesn't emerge in a vacuum. Americans overall are deeply conflicted—and divided—about the relationship between the market and the state. A 2018 survey from the Gallup organization found that "for the 12th year in a row, more Americans say there is 'too much' government regulation of business and industry (39%) than say there is either 'too little' (25%) or 'the right amount' (33%)."[5] Gallup also found that 68 percent of Republicans think there is too much regulation versus only 20 percent of Democrats.[6] This partisan divide was found also in a survey by the Pew Research Center, noting that "the divisions between Republicans and Democrats on fundamental political values—on government, race, immigration, national security, environmental protection and other areas—reached record levels during Barack Obama's presidency. In Donald Trump's first year as president, these gaps have grown even larger."[7] And yet the Cato Institute (which tends to advocate for less regulation of the market) conducted a survey that found that 59 percent of Americans "believe regulations, at least in the past, have produced positive benefits" and 56 percent believe that "regulations can help make businesses more responsive to people's needs."[8]

### THE GROWING CORPORATE INFLUENCE IN POLITICS

When looking at the seeming contradictions in these surveys, Karlyn Bowman at *Forbes* concluded that "we want to get government off the back of business, but at the same time, we want to be protected" from excessive corporate greed and abuse.[9] For as much as Americans distrust the involvement of government in the market, they are also wary of the special interests and lobbying that have distorted our democratic processes. Indeed, a 2014 study by the political scientists Martin Gilens of Princeton and Benjamin Page of Northwestern concluded that economic elites and narrow interest groups were very influential in the establishment and form of federal policy between 1981 and 2002 while the views of ordinary citizens had virtually no independent effect at all, concluding that "the preferences of the average American appear to have only a minuscule near-zero, statistically non-significant impact upon public policy."[10] That conclusion would seem to be supported by the amount of money that is spent on lobbying each year, reaching $3.4 billion in 2018, with the US Chamber of Commerce topping the list at $95 million followed by the National Association of Realtors at $73 million and the Pharmaceutical Research and Manufacturers of America at $28 million.[11] Of the $1.3 billion spent by super PACs in the 2018 election cycle, corporations in the finance, insurance, and real estate sectors gave a combined $595 million.[12] And corporate executives also give as individuals; casino magnate Sheldon Adelson singlehandedly gave over $100 million to political candidates in 2018.[13]

There is good reason to be concerned about the extent to which corporations influence policy, especially when they lobby for or against certain policies, often while offering public statements to the contrary. InfluenceMap, a watchdog organization that tracks corporate influence, for example found that the largest oil and gas companies spend nearly $200 million per year in lobbying efforts to delay, control, or block policies to tackle climate change.[14] All totaled, the level of corporate influence is straining government's ability to set even the most rudimentary policies on income inequality (such as tax reform, worker training, or health care) or climate change (for example, a carbon price).

Today's business students, then, are entering a world where distrust of the relationship between business and government is at all-time highs. At the same time, many corporations enjoy tremendous power to lobby governments in ways that are often in opposition to public interest, and few business schools offer courses on how to make the relationship between business and government better to improve society. Fewer still bring together students and faculty from the schools of business and public policy to debate the issue and reach more productive outcomes.

A good starting point for this conversation would be a constructive debate about lobbying. Public perceptions of lobbying are generally negative, seeing it as either inappropriate influence of business in the policy domain (that is, government capture) or an unwarranted intrusion of government in the market (that is, crony capitalism or "picking winners and losers"). But this is not how lobbying has to work. Lobbying is basic to democratic politics as governments seek guidance on how to set the rules of the market and usher reforms as needed. Common and convenient stereotypes of lobbyists as cigar-smoking fat-cats making backroom deals aside, many lobbyists are well-informed and conscientious individuals providing a valuable service to government. In fact, talk to any good lobbyist and they will tell you that gaining trust and acting with integrity are central to their ability to do their job.

There are many examples of corporate lobbying serving the public interest. In 2006, for example, Mary Kay lobbied for the Violence Against Women Act as well as for insurance coverage for mammograms, rural screening programs, and an increase in research on breast cancer. In 2001, Levi Strauss & Co. lobbied the Guatemalan Minister of Labor to strengthen his country's labor laws and improve workers' standards of living. In 1997, Cascade Engineering lobbied the state of Michigan to invest more funds in "welfare-to-career" programs.[15]

In recognition of the shared interest that government and business have in solving society's deepest and most systemic challenges, business education needs to teach more examples like these and reformulate ideas about lobbying as a public service that upholds obligations toward the collective good and not just individual gamesmanship. But business schools also need to encourage students to think hard about how to counter the negative lobbying that corrodes our democracy.

That may mean introducing them to the work of people such as business economics professor Tom Lyon at the University of Michigan, who has been doing research for years on corporate greenwashing, the practice of publicly supporting sustainability while privately acting otherwise. He is particularly focused on the disconnect between public statements and lobbying efforts, warning that this is so easy to get away with because it's hard to detect corporate lobbying efforts as there is no requirement to disclose them.[16] Exxon-Mobil, for example, states on its webpage, "We are committed to positive action on climate change,"[17] while spending over $40 million in 2018 to lobby against climate policies,[18] and has supported trade groups like the American Legislative Exchange Council (ALEC) and the American Petroleum Institute (API), who also lobbied against climate policy. To expose such double strategies, Lyon and his coauthors call for regulation that requires that corporations disclose more details about their political actions, both individually and as part of industry associations, make their lobbying stances public, and reveal which politicians they have called on to take a given position.[19]

In fact, this may not be such a radically new idea. Some people may be surprised to know that many forms of lobbying were banned through the nineteenth century in the United States. The Georgia state constitution at one time read that "lobbying is declared to be a crime," and in California, it was a felony. It was not until the early 1970s that major corporations began to lobby aggressively on their own behalf.[20] From then on, the corrupting influence of self-interest began to pick up.

### THE ACTIVIST CEO

There is another reason to begin serious discussion and education about the respective roles of business and government. Regardless of people's distrust of business, companies are stepping into the civic domain more directly as the "activist CEO" grows in prominence. Numerous corporations took an active role in opposing anti–gay marriage legislation in Indiana, Georgia, and North Carolina.[21] Delta challenged the National Rifle Association in the wake of mass shootings by curtailing flight discounts to its members. Blackrock and JP Morgan instituted de facto sanctions on Saudi Arabia after the Jamal Khashoggi murder by canceling participation in important meetings in country[22] (however, they resumed their participation the following year). Hobby Lobby sued the federal government to be exempt from providing contraception to its employees under the Affordable Care Act on grounds that this violated its religious beliefs.[23]

In such cases, executives are pushed into action by circumstances (for example, Sanofi, maker of Ambien, had to issue a press release to challenge Roseanne Barr's charge that the drug caused her to make a series of racist tweets, which in turn led to her ABC sitcom being cancelled[24]); by their own employees (for example, Microsoft employees demanded the company cancel its contract with the Immigration and Customs Enforcement agency in protest over the Trump administration's zero tolerance policy on immigration[25]); or by straight business self-interest. But while we may cheer these efforts when they align with our values and jeer when they are not, the real issue is that these corporate executives were not elected, nor are they held accountable as public servants. They have an unavoidable conflict of interest when such actions have a clear profit implication for their companies. Therefore, activist CEOs can never be fully honest brokers, as they have a financial stake in the policy debates in which they engage and will be less sympathetic to actions that serve the public good but do not make a profit.[26]

## THE BLURRING LINE BETWEEN BUSINESS AND GOVERNMENT

The actions of executives and their companies is blurring the line between business and government. Or, more to the point, they are displacing the role of government, while also simultaneously criticizing government for being ineffective. This is not democracy. As today's corporate executives denigrate government breakdown, future business leaders should be trained to ask how corporations have contributed to that breakdown through their lobbying efforts and their ability to avoid paying corporate income taxes—in 2018, just over ninety profitable Fortune 500 companies paid zero federal income taxes.[27]

Even within the business community, some are clashing over the proper roles of business and government. While the Business Roundtable garnered a great deal of positive press in 2019 for its statement that the corporation must serve more than just the shareholder, the Council of Institutional Investors warned that this is not their role but that of the government, issuing a statement that "accountability to everyone means accountability to no one. It is government, not companies that should shoulder the responsibility of defining and addressing societal objectives with limited or no connection to long-term shareholder value."[28]

There is no clear or easy answer to these debates, which is why we must begin teaching today's business students to engage in them more thoughtfully and constructively. In the end, capitalism is a set of institutions for structuring our commerce and interaction. It is not, as some think, a sort of natural state that exists free from government regulation. It is designed by human beings in the service of human beings, and it is designed to evolve. The idea that we can have a functioning and effective market without government is naïve. As Jerry Taylor, president of the libertarian Niskanen Center, wrote, "Wherever we look around the world, when we see inconsequential governments with limited power, as libertarians would prefer, we see 'failed states.' How much liberty and human dignity can be found there? Very little."[29] The question is not whether there is or is not a role for government in the market. The question is how government can and will evolve side by side with the market to help us address the challenges we face as a society.

CHAPTER 6

# DEMOCRACY AND THE MARKETPLACE

**THE BLURRING OF BUSINESS** and government described in the previous chapter has an effect on society that goes well beyond the halls of government. It is changing our culture. Many in this country are turning away from the values of democracy, and turning toward the values of the market in guiding our thinking in the civic sphere. Importantly, many don't know the difference, viewing capitalism and democracy as one and the same. This is a grave error. And to see that error we can turn to the wisdom of James Madison, an influential contributor to the drafting of the US Constitution and the fourth president of the United States.[1]

But first, I want to pose a provocative question. How many Americans know that we live in a "representative democracy" or a republic, that this is what the founding fathers wanted, or even what that means? Those applying for US citizenship are taught this, as it is spelled out on the US Citizenship and Immigration Service webpage: "The United States is a representative democracy. This means that our government is elected by citizens. Here, citizens vote for their government officials. These officials represent the citizens' ideas and concerns in government."[2] James Madison wrote that the role of representative democracy (or republic) is to

> refine and enlarge the public views, by passing them through the medium
> of a chosen body of citizens, whose wisdom may best discern the true

interest of their country, and whose patriotism and love of justice will be least likely to sacrifice it to temporary or partial considerations. *Federalist Paper* No. 10 (1787)

Nowhere in these statements is there any suggestion that every citizen's view is equally valid or that democracy exists to serve the majority. And yet, that seems to be an increasingly prevalent view in our society. It is a view that is driven by market values—if enough people want to buy a product, it has value; the majority rules. For example, many critics argue that universities should not exercise control over who speaks on their campuses, claiming that the market should decide such matters: "If no one comes to hear him speak, society will have spoken." But should that always be true? Is any speech, even racist or hate speech, open to the verdict of the market? This issue came to the fore when universities began to reevaluate their speaker policies over white nationalist Richard Spencer, a man who by his own admission seeks to rile the campus and challenge the status quo.[3] Should university administrators have no say against the logic of the market? In 2017, a woman was killed at a Spencer rally at the University of Virginia in which white nationalist marchers chanted "Jews will not replace us."[4] In 2019, violence broke out between white nationalists and antifascist protesters at his speech at Michigan State University.[5] In cases like these, the market may have determined that Spencer's incendiary rhetoric has value, at least for some. The only option available to Florida governor Rick Scott in advance of a Spencer speech at the University of Florida was to declare a state of emergency.

We can also see this market logic of majority rules play out in what elected politics is becoming. With district boundaries manipulated to favor one party through gerrymandering and policy positions often decided by polling and focus groups, politicians seek only to satisfy "their" constituent majority and operate under a false perception that they should not engage with alternative views. It is becoming less important for politicians to consider many sides of an issue, negotiate with those who see the issues differently, and seek compromised solutions that serve all of society. If an issue becomes too thorny to handle, politicians then turn it over to the general public through referenda, which warps the intended function of government even further, as the battle becomes one not of ideas and public interest but of large and competing pocketbooks. In 2018, more than $1.1 billion was spent in support of and opposition to statewide ballot measures across the United States.[6] That year, California's Proposition 8—which would have limited dialysis clinic profits to 15 percent above service costs—set a record for campaign spending with opponents (mostly dialysis centers and their trade associations) putting an astonishing $111.4 million into the fight while proponents could only muster $18 million.[7] The proposition failed, as would be expected by simply looking at the size of the competing expenditures.

In 2018, Taiwan held a public referendum to approve same-sex marriage, and political leaders were shocked when the country voted "no" even though their courts had previously ruled that limiting marriage to heterosexual couples was unconstitutional. This result was the product of a well-funded campaign by conservative Christian groups, much of it based on misinformation (such as warning of an AIDS epidemic).[8] Is this a democratic process that reflects the will of an informed electorate? No. The minority was oppressed by a majority that was misguided by big-money advertising. James Madison might have been appalled but not surprised:

> Where a majority are united by a common sentiment, and have an opportunity, the rights of the minor party become insecure. *Madison Debates* (1787)

By turning democracy over to the market, we give in to a logic that is indifferent to the social value or worth of the outcome. The market is indifferent to the merit of a product—pet rock, radar detector, tobacco, pornography. It is indifferent to those who don't buy the product, even those who may oppose it. It cares only about profit; if enough consumers buy it, it has merit, regardless of whether those consumers benefit from the product, need it, or are even harmed by it. For example, in 2019 the Michigan Court of Claims stopped the state's ban on flavored vapes aimed at youths, arguing that the economic harm done to vape businesses by the ban outweighed the health and safety interests of the people, even though teen vaping had been linked to serious health risks and several deaths. The market will never ask you to sacrifice for the greater good, focusing instead on your immediate and selfish needs. The will of the majority, the mob, will never lead to a stable democracy. This unhealthy logic is heading toward something even more sinister as the mentality of the market spreads further into our society.

## AMPLIFYING THE LOGIC OF THE MARKET
## TO THE WHIMS OF THE MOB

While the logic of the market is taking over the civic sphere, social media are making things worse as politicians (and journalists) use Twitter retweets and Facebook likes as proxies of public opinion, and the public uses social media as a venue for civic discourse. Both common sense and rigorous research show that social media do not reflect the concerns and interests of the overall public.[9] Between 15 percent[10] and 66 percent[11] of all Tweets come from bots, and what remains is dominated by a minority of loud and vocal people. But the hostile and sensational tone of the content this medium produces affects our thinking and behavior in some negative ways. Social media facilitate a mob mentality[12] that encourages antisocial behavior through detachment and anonymity.[13]

The field of mob psychology explains that mobs usually assemble after an act of perceived inequality or unfairness, and the strong communal emotion can make the cause seem even more important. The collective response can be active or passive, the former being a mob and the latter an audience. But it is the mob that seems to be taking over in social media, making us ruder and meaner in the process.[14] Once triggered by some strong emotion cue, we join the anonymity of the internet, experience a loss of self-awareness, and are less likely to follow normal restraints and inhibitions.[15] This experience can generate a sense of emotional excitement, but it leads to the provocation of behaviors that a person would not typically engage in if alone.

In one of the more extreme cases of Twitter rage, Justine Sacco, the senior director of corporate communications at IAC, became the number one trend on Twitter in 2013 after she posted a joke that was in poor taste and then boarded her flight to South Africa. In the course of her flight, the hashtag #HasJustineLandedYet went global and tens of thousands of tweets attacked and mocked her. When she landed, a Twitter user took her picture and posted it online, co-workers shunned her, and she was eventually fired. She became the poster child for "Twitter shaming,"[16] but she is not alone. Many who study and speak about climate change have experienced anonymous and aggressive social media attacks for their work. I have received hate mail that expresses views that I have never been told in person: "you are working for Satan," "Are you an idiot deceiver or just plain [sic] stupid?", "please by all means, just kill yourself!", and "Hey Dick Head. Sorry you have such an empty life, but I'm going to bet it gets a lot worse from here."

Research by Mina Cikara and Rebecca Saxe finds that "although humans exhibit strong preferences for equity and moral prohibitions against harm in many contexts, people's priorities change when there is an 'us' and a 'them,'" and they lose touch with their personal moral code.[17] In such ways, the mob can be incited, but it is hard to control or contain once stirred. While social media can lead to organized and peaceful demonstration, "Twitter storms" or "social media outrage" increasingly drive our social discourse when the over-riding mode is outrage, incivility, and zealotry, often based on incomplete or incorrect information.

These behaviors and emotional perspectives are not conducive to the kind of tempered, thorough, and compromise-seeking discourse that democratic government needs in order to function well. It is far easier to express your feelings from the privacy of your computer than it is to do the hard work of engaging in democracy. Social media will never be a replacement for the civic commons of face-to-face communication, traditional media, town hall meetings, public debates, and careful reflection. These media are all too often driven by a logic of the mob that signifies our increasingly market-driven democracy by equating the volume of retweets or likes with the merit of the argument.

### DEMOCRACY AS "FARCE OR TRAGEDY OR PERHAPS BOTH"?

Roger McNamee, an early investor in Facebook, warned in 2019 that Facebook, Google, and other tech giants represent "the greatest threat to the global order in my lifetime."[18] Though he profited from his investments, McNamee began to see the more sinister ways in which "democracy has been undermined because of design choices" that include the Facebook platform's pleasurable, frictionless interface, which encourages users to stay, return, and essentially crave the process of "likes" and "tags" as an artificial surrogate for human interaction. It has increasingly become an open platform to disseminate dangerous and destructive ideas, and it is this corrosive impact on the quality of social and political discourse that has led McNamee to advocate for breaking up Facebook's data monopoly by force, and heavily regulating its business practices.

The RAND Corporation calls the current reality of misinformation and disinformation "truth decay," in which we disagree about facts and increasingly blur opinion and fact, an unprecedented reality that poses an existential threat to our democracy.[19] Their report argues, "The most damaging effects might be the erosion of civil discourse, political paralysis, alienation and disengagement of individuals from political and civic institutions, and uncertainty about U.S. policy." James Madison might agree:

> A popular government without popular information or the means of acquiring it is but a prologue to farce or tragedy or perhaps both. Knowledge will forever govern ignorance, and a people who mean to be their own Governors must arm themselves with the power knowledge gives." Letter to W. T. Barry (1822)

There is no simple answer to deal with the existential threat created by the potent and destructive combination of market logic, mob mentality, hostile social media, and weakened democracy. While government policy can seek to break up or reign in Facebook, and Twitter can self-regulate by choosing to eliminate political ads in the 2020 presidential election, what we can do as individual citizens is identify the problem, revisit the basic values of our democracy, and attempt to rectify the situation in our sphere of influence.

We can begin by challenging our politicians to strive for their better selves and model the behavior we want from them by getting outside the filter bubbles created by social media and selectively chosen news sources, finding information sources that cross the political spectrum, seeking out and engaging people who think differently, debating our neighbors with civility, and, above all, learning to compromise and to protect the interests of the minority against the majority. In short, we simply need to relearn how to exercise our roles as citizens, a role whose very retreat will destroy our democracy.

I see too many business students who strive to make a difference in the world only through the economic sphere—start a business, create a new app, or influence the clout of a large corporation—without taking into consideration how they fit into the wider public sphere. These entrepreneurial ventures are valuable activities, but they must not preclude business leaders' roles as citizens and in the process add one more brick to the wall of market democracy. If business students and leaders are disengaging from government, government will continue to be demoted as an irrelevant and ineffective force in society. And as that continues, democracy is further eroded. We need to bring the lessons of James Madison and others into the core of business education to help students understand the many roles that business can play within the broader society of which they are a part, and ultimately steer business toward the one that is in society's best long-term interests.

# CHAPTER 7

# LEARNING THE VALUE OF GOVERNMENT IN THE WAKE OF A SHUTDOWN

IN 2019, the United States endured the longest government shutdown in its history, lasting thirty-five days, and Americans got a taste of life without government. The absence of some services was clearly visible, such as a buildup of trash at national parks (such as Sequoia and Kings Canyon National Parks)[1] or longer lines at airport security checkpoints.[2] Others were less noticeable but just as important, such as an inability of entrepreneurs to get small business loans[3] or limited service from the Internal Revenue Service, the Securities and Exchange Commission, and other key agencies.

Many Americans realized, some perhaps for the first time, that government matters. But once the shutdown ended and the memories of the pain and discomfort it caused began to fade, the visceral reminder Americans got of this message faded with it, as it did when Americans forgot or underestimated the damage of the sixteen-day 2013 shutdown.[4] Yet it's essential that we not forget, and the shutdown provides a good opportunity to reflect on the government's vital role in the free market and to think about how we might find a better balance between regulation and business.[5]

## HOW THE SHUTDOWN AFFECTED BUSINESS

The shutdown of 2019 left about eight hundred thousand government employees either furloughed or working without pay, affecting more than ten agencies.[6] This resulted in the slowing or halting of a great deal of economic activity, including food safety inspections,[7] initial public offerings on the stock market,[8] and even the approval of new craft beers.[9]

And these costs were felt by citizens as the risks grew to their food,[10] the environment,[11] and other important aspects of their daily life. Economists warned that long-term impacts could also undermine market confidence, as businesses, consumers, and investors might begin to lose faith in political leaders' ability to make constructive policies. White House economists estimated that every week of being shutdown reduced growth by 0.13 percentage points,[12] meaning that the costs to the economy exceeded $6 billion, which is more than what President Trump was demanding for a border wall, which is what precipitated the shutdown in the first place.[13]

### HAMILTON AND PUBLIC GOODS

While the shutdown crystallized what the absence of government feels like, its massive costs triggered debate over the government's proper role in the market. This debate is as old as the American Republic. For example, Alexander Hamilton, the nation's first Treasury secretary, wrote eloquently about the need for the government to get involved in markets, specifically through the establishment of a national bank, which he called a key public institution that "facilitates and extends the operations of commerce among individuals. Industry is increased, commodities are multiplied, agriculture and manufacturers flourish: and herein consists the true wealth and prosperity of a state."[14]

The role of government in the market goes far beyond just a central bank. "Public goods" often require the protection of a set of laws. Examples include the environment, national defense, national parks, consumer protection, and advanced research that helps seed inventions and create the industries of our future.

Author Michael Lewis, in his book *The Fifth Risk*, detailed many of the important yet little-noticed functions that government agencies handle well in the market.[15] For example, on issues such as the protection of food safety or the oversight of spent nuclear resources, government can look beyond immediate and individual profit concerns and consider the greater collective good and a time horizon that goes beyond the short-term thinking of the quarterly return or stock portfolio. Further, he showed how a functioning economy depends on civil servants using the best data and science available to provide vital services to all Americans. Lewis pointed out that government scientists have long been mining these data to protect Americans, but a lot of government data had begun disappearing from government websites around the time of the shutdown (such as data on climate change at the EPA, animal abuse at the Department of Agriculture, or violent crime at the Department of Justice), and he warned, "Under each act of data suppression, usually lay a narrow commercial motive: a gun lobbyist, a coal company, a poultry company."

To offer just one example of the federal government's positive role in the market, we can look at the level of innovation that was spurred by the Defense Advanced Research Projects Agency (DARPA). Created in 1957 under the Department of Defense to develop emerging technologies for use by the military, many of its products have been made available to the general public through the market. Among them, DARPA gave us the internet, GPS, stealth aircraft, and countless other technologies used in nondefense sectors today.[16]

On the flip side, the absence of proper regulation can lead to serious economic and personal damage, as experienced during the global financial crisis in 2008 that was caused in part by the repeal of the Glass-Steagall Act. That Act was passed in the aftermath of the Great Depression in the 1930s to separate commercial banking from investment banking and provide for safeguards against too much leverage and excessive risk taking. But once the act was repealed in 1999 after lobbying from the financial sector, Wall Street banks immediately started to consolidate, leading to the phenomenon of the "too big to fail" financial institutions in which the investment arm could take much larger risks with money collected in the banking arm.

And only government—through regulatory agencies and smartly designed laws—is in a position to prevent another crisis. In the words of Aaron Klein at the Brookings Institution, a former chief economist for the Senate Banking Committee, "We have made substantial progress in building a safer and more resilient financial system since the [2008] crisis. Changes in law like Dodd-Frank created a stronger regulatory system and gave regulators new tools to detect, prevent, and contain future problems. These reforms can make future crises less likely to occur and mitigate the impact when they do."[17]

And yet fears have been growing that another financial crisis may be on the horizon as a result of Wall Street excesses and financial bubbles in housing and debt. Global debt rose to a record $247 trillion in the first quarter of 2019, far higher than the $177.8 trillion in the pre-crisis first quarter of 2008,[18] and economist and Nobel Laureate Robert Shiller warned that the housing market is in another bubble phase—"It's like 2005 again"—with the San Francisco and Los Angeles markets already slowing down.[19] The point is that in all these cases, the question is not about whether or not government should be involved in the market, but about how much, in what way, and at which level (local, state, or federal). But as we learned in the shutdown, the absence of government and its regulatory oversight can lead to market excesses and market failures.

## AMERICANS' EVOLVING VIEWS

Americans are increasingly abandoning the view that government should stay out of business and the market and are embracing the idea of an expanded role for the public sector. While more Americans still think that there is too much regulation rather than not enough, that number has declined from 50 percent in 2011 to 39 percent in 2018, the lowest in a decade according to Gallup—with a growing share saying that the balance is "just right" (up from 23 percent to 33 percent in the same time period).[20] This comes at a time when the Trump administration is boasting about the number of regulations it has eliminated.[21]

These surveys suggest Americans don't simply want fewer regulations, they want better ones. One area in which people see value in increased government regulation is the financial sector, which is viewed by many as rapacious and in need of more monitoring. A Cato Institute survey from 2017 found that 77 percent believe bankers would harm consumers if they thought they could make a lot of money doing so and get away with it; 64 percent think Wall Street bankers "get paid huge amounts of money" for "essentially tricking people"; and 49 percent worry that corruption in the industry is "widespread" rather than limited to a few institutions. [22]

## TOWARD A BETTER BALANCE

Unfortunately, instead of a debate over the right balance for government, American politicians and others have denigrated government as "the problem" (President Reagan in 1981) or "the swamp" (President Trump in 2016). The terms are meant to suggest that government is alternatively inept, obstructive, or corrupt. These politicians do this to take advantage of the widespread misperception that government has no role in markets and that regulation represents an unwarranted intrusion on business. While there certainly are problems with special interest influence in government and with bureaucratic inefficiency, as indicated in the previous chapter, the enterprise as a whole remains central to the operation of capitalism and the markets.

After all, capitalism is a set of institutions designed by government in concert with business and civil society. As *National Affairs* editor Yuval Levin points out, even Adam Smith, the Scottish economist who wrote the foundational texts on capitalism, argued that "the rules of the market are not self-legislating or naturally obvious."[23] Rather, Smith said, the market is a public institution that requires rules imposed upon it by legislators who understand its workings and its benefits.

So it is time to return to the basics and teach business leaders about the importance of "reinventing government" to improve how the various branches and levels interact with each other and the market.[24] At the same time, it's important to provide more business education on what government does, and invite business students into the conversation about how to do it better—including at the ballot box.

CHAPTER 8

# FIGHTING CLIMATE
# CHANGE TOGETHER

YALE ECONOMIST William Nordhaus has devoted his life's work to understanding the costs of climate change and advocating the use of a carbon tax
to curb global warming. It was no small irony, then, that on October 8, 2018,
the same day his research shared in the Nobel Prize in Economic Sciences,
a United Nations panel released its latest report on the mounting dangers of
climate change.[1] In fact, the report built upon much of Nordhaus's work and
warned that we have until 2030 to keep temperatures below 1.5 degrees Celsius to avoid environmental catastrophe.

This warning—and the award—came at a time when many Americans were
not listening. The US had pulled out of the Paris Accord to address climate
change, a broad swath of the country still denied the existence of the problem,
and some policymakers at the state and federal levels refused to incorporate
climate science into their decision making. North Carolina legislators, for example, voted in 2012 to ban any state agencies from making policies on sea-level
change, even though such studies showed that seas could rise as much as thirty-
nine inches by 2100.[2] In Florida, Department of Environmental Protection
officials were ordered in 2015 not to use the terms "climate change" or "global
warming" in any official communications, emails, or reports.[3] And the Federal
Emergency Management Agency has continued to pay to rebuild after flood
damage despite increased warnings that flooding will continue.[4]

But Nordhaus's work is not about whether or not people and policymakers
"believe" in climate change. It's about how the market, when guided by the

government, has an ability to address the most serious issue facing humanity in this century. His research offers hope that business leaders—and indeed all citizens—can help prevent global calamity.[5]

## THE ECONOMICS OF CLIMATE CHANGE

One of Nordhaus's most significant contributions was his ability to unpack and explain the complex issues surrounding climate change. In his book *Climate Casino*, for example, Nordhaus explained the many interrelated topics when talking about climate change, from science and energy to economics and politics, while clearly identifying the steps necessary to prevent catastrophe.[6] Or as the *New York Times* put it, "It is a one-stop source on global warming, seen through the prism of a brilliant economist."[7] Although his writing was accessible, he showed that he was still grappling with the uncertainty of his and other projections, allowing people to see the honest complexity of outcomes related to how humans harm the environment through greenhouse gas emissions.

## MODELING THE ECONOMY AND CLIMATE

A key premise of Nordhaus's research is that the environment is a public good, shared by all and yet not paid for in any adequate or appropriate way. In other words, we all benefit from it, though we don't necessarily pay for it. In fact, a 1997 research study in *Nature* calculated the value of free services that the $18 trillion world economy receives from the environment at between $16 and $54 trillion per year, with a likely figure of at least $33 trillion.[8] We are all harmed by the environment's degradation, even though the value of that damage is not captured in standard market exchange.

Nordhaus argued that a tax on carbon—say, $25 a ton—or a cap-and-trade scheme that allows companies to exchange pollution credits, offers the best and most economically efficient way of putting a value on that public good and thus doing something about the problem. Nordhaus showed this by perfecting models that simulated how such taxes and other inputs affect both the economy and the climate, depicting how they co-evolve—known as "integrated assessment" models.[9] A noteworthy example is his Dynamic Integrated Climate-Economy (DICE) model, which provides a consistent framework for using knowledge borne from economics, ecology, and the earth sciences.[10] The model allowed for a deeper understanding of how certain policy changes affect long-term economic and environmental outcomes.

This is how he realized that schemes that rely on markets with some guidance from governments—such as by instituting carbon taxes—would work best to tackle the problem. And thus he was able to show, with great clarity, that the most cost effective way to reduce greenhouse gas emissions is by lifting the price of fossil fuels with a carbon tax. This in turn would provide the appropriate incentives for consumers and businesses to use less of those fuels and find alternatives. Nordhaus was also able to estimate that the economic damage from climate change if such policies were not adopted would have a present-discounted value of $22.5 trillion by 2100.[11] He found that the people who would lose the most were the poor and those living in tropical regions. Certainly his work leads to the conclusion that the economic and moral case for action far exceeds the case for inaction. It also shows how capitalism is capable of rising to the challenge of climate change, just as it has to other problems in the marketplace, such as ozone depletion and acid rain.

## MARKETS AND A GUIDING HAND

In a time when the world's leading scientists have issued dire warnings on the impending crisis of climate change, Nordhaus's deeply thoughtful, methodical work is a reminder that there is hope that human ingenuity and resourcefulness can guide policy and the market to a coordinated solution and a better form of capitalism for structuring our commerce and interaction.

Business education must include thorough coverage of such a coordinated role of government in the market. While the current public and political debate over collusion between government and large corporations, "crony capitalism," and unfair competition leads to questions of more versus less government, business education should focus on the search for a balanced and collaborative level of business-government engagement. In proposing ways to amend capitalism's flaws, Joseph Stiglitz wrote, "The prescription follows from the diagnosis: It begins by recognizing the vital role that the state plays in making markets serve society. . . . Markets don't exist in a vacuum; they have to be structured by rules and regulations, and those rules and regulations must be enforced."[12] The development of those rules and regulations has been and will continue to be influenced by corporations and the executives that lead them. Therefore future business leaders must be taught to think of government influence in general, and lobbying in particular, as a service in the interests of making a fair, equitable, and sustainable economy for all and not just the wealthy few.[13]

PART 3

# COMMUNICATING CHANGE

# CHAPTER 9

# COMMUNICATING IN POLITICALLY CHARGED ENVIRONMENTS

I HAVE FOUND that organizational change management is one of the least popular courses among business students and one of the most popular in executive education. Too many students think that they just have to come up with the right idea and they have done their work. Executives know that the hard part is convincing people it is the right thing to do and then getting them to do it. When it comes to addressing environmental and social issues, that task becomes even more difficult.

Since 1997, PwC has been conducting its annual Global CEO survey, a survey of over thirteen hundred chief executives in more than ninety territories that explores expectations, priorities, and concerns for both their business and the global business climate in the coming year. Climate change dropped from ninth place in 2018 to thirteenth in 2019 in terms of perceived threats to an organization's growth prospects.[1] It was superseded by concerns for over-regulation (first), policy uncertainty (second), availability of key skills (third), trade conflicts (fourth), and cyber threats (fifth). Only 38 percent of CEOs felt that data about the impact of climate change on the business were critical or important for decision making, and only 17 percent felt the data were comprehensive as currently received. The 2019 report concluded that "CEOs are less bothered by the broad, existential threats that figured prominently in the rankings last year, like terrorism and climate change." This lack of concern was voiced by Warren Buffet when he said, "I don't think in making an investment decision on Berkshire Hathaway, or most companies—virtually all of the companies I can think of—that climate change should be a factor in the decision-making process."[2]

Why is there such a professed lack of concern over climate change, given the massive financial threats it poses to businesses and their leaders (registered notably by insurance companies, as discussed in Chapter 4)? To begin, many CEOs and board members are not well versed in science, and an often underlooked reason for that is that scientists have not done a good job of communicating to the public. Either they are staying out of the public and political debates, preferring to remain within their narrow research communities, or, when they do stray outside the ivory tower, they adopt a tone and posture that fails to reach its intended lay audience. The same could be said for business leaders as they attempt to convey their concerns to the general public.

## RECOGNIZE THE HUMAN AND EMOTIONAL
## ASPECTS OF COMMUNICATION

In fact, both scientists and business leaders often adopt what is called the "knowledge deficit model" when speaking to the public—the idea that people's brains are only half full and if they merely pour their knowledge into them, people will think like they do and make the right decisions. That is obviously an exaggeration, but it holds a kernel of truth. I see too many people approach the public sphere with a tone of condescension, backed up by data, but ignoring the human and emotional aspects of public controversies. As a result, other interests who are able to capture that human aspect of the issues win the hearts and minds of people because they relate to them on a different level, recognizing their concerns and communicating in a way that reaches them where they are. I see this happen when coal miners or conservative radio show hosts argue that climate science is a hoax and that it will destroy jobs while scientists argue concentrations, radiative forcing, and long-term projections. And I see it happen when nonprofits argue that corporate actions will destroy communities while executives argue about financial projections, return on investment, and economic analysis.

Instead, scientists and business executives would do well to begin engaging the public with the questions "What are your concerns? How can I help?" It requires one to strike the right tone and posture so as to be heard. And that means that engagement must be more than a one-way communication. To be truly effective, one needs to both listen and speak, to profess topic knowledge but also express humility and patience in hearing what people need and what they want. Everyone could benefit from such an approach.

I have long thought about science communication in terms of bridging worlds that don't know how to talk with or understand one another. For example, when I look at data like those in Figure 6, depicting the wide gaps between scientists and the general public on a variety of scientific issues, I have always seen a form of communication breakdown.

But in some cases, this framing is not quite right. At times, the gap is created not by a lack of understating but by an open resentment; the public is deaf to the conclusions of the scientific community, not because they don't understand science or the scientific community, but because they actively don't like how they are treated by scientists. It's an issue of tone and respect. There are some within the scientific community who view the public in low regard (perhaps because they themselves have been treated with disrespect by that public). There are others who subscribe to a view of scientism that elevates the natural sciences in relation to all other ways of knowing the world around us and holds "the view that the characteristic inductive methods of the natural sciences are the only source of genuine factual knowledge and, in particular, that they alone can yield true knowledge about man and society."[3] People who hold such views are often dismissive of the arts, the humanities, religion, and pragmatic experience as ways to know and understand the natural world, and they can be quite aggressive in expressing that dismissive attitude. The American Association for the Advancement of Science (AAAS) points out that "with scientism, you will regularly hear explanations that rely on words like 'merely,' 'only,' 'simply,' or 'nothing more than.' Scientism restricts human inquiry." One example the AAAS highlights is a quote from nineteenth-century social theorist Henri de Saint-Simon: "A scientist, my dear friends, is a man who foresees; it is because science provides the means to predict that it is useful, and the scientists are superior to all other men."[4]

But this arrogance and restriction of human inquiry only partly explains why some members of the public still do not accept the conclusions of scientists and business people, particularly on the issue of climate change. It must be noted that significant funding for miscommunication has been added to the public debate. Robert Brulle, professor of sociology and environmental science at Drexel University, examined how ninety-one corporations, think tanks, and advocacy groups of the "climate change counter movement" (CCCM) enjoyed a total annual income of just over $900 million and collectively received more than $7 billion between 2003 and 2010 from conservative foundations to challenge climate science.[5] The motivations of this movement center on issues such

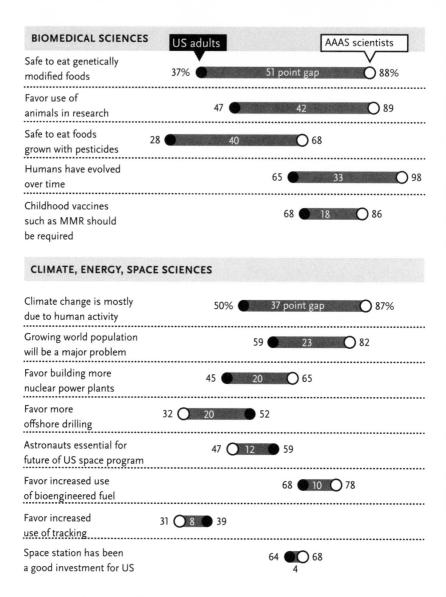

**BIOMEDICAL SCIENCES** | US adults | AAAS scientists

Safe to eat genetically modified foods — 37% | 51 point gap | 88%

Favor use of animals in research — 47 | 42 | 89

Safe to eat foods grown with pesticides — 28 | 40 | 68

Humans have evolved over time — 65 | 33 | 98

Childhood vaccines such as MMR should be required — 68 | 18 | 86

**CLIMATE, ENERGY, SPACE SCIENCES**

Climate change is mostly due to human activity — 50% | 37 point gap | 87%

Growing world population will be a major problem — 59 | 23 | 82

Favor building more nuclear power plants — 45 | 20 | 65

Favor more offshore drilling — 32 | 20 | 52

Astronauts essential for future of US space program — 47 | 12 | 59

Favor increased use of bioengineered fuel — 68 | 10 | 78

Favor increased use of tracking — 31 | 8 | 39

Space station has been a good investment for US — 64 | 4 | 68

FIGURE 6 Opinion Differences Between the Public and Scientists: Percentage of US Adults and AAAS Scientists Agreeing with Each Statement. Notes: Survey of US adults August 15–25, 2014. AAAS scientist survey September 11–October 13, 2014. Other responses and those saying "don't know" or giving no answer are not shown. Source: C. Funk, L. Rainie, and D. Page, *Public and scientists' views on science and society* (Washington, DC: Pew Research Center, 2015), used with permission.

as protecting freedom and defending the market against excessive control, socialism, and communism. Whitney Ball, chief executive of the Donors Trust, a libertarian nonprofit that is one of the largest funders of the CCCM, said that "we exist to help donors promote liberty which we understand to be limited government, personal responsibility and free enterprise."[6] Some conservative groups see climate policy as a covert way for the government to interfere in the market and diminish citizens' liberty. For many there is a belief that climate change is inextricably tied to a liberal political ideology that borders on socialism.[7] In the words of one speaker at the climate-change-skeptic Heartland Conference, climate change believers "hate people, they hate the Western economy." Another went further to suggest, "He who controls carbon controls life," and told the audience that Americans might end up with carbon rationing cards for every person if climate believers succeed.[8]

These groups are not engaged in a scientific debate over carbon dioxide and greenhouse gas models. They are protecting some deeply held values that they believe are under attack. While the numbers are dwindling—the percentage of Americans who deny that climate change is happening dropped from 41 percent in 2010 to 29 percent in 2017[9]—their resistance to what they see as a "hoax" is deep.

## AVOID TERMS LADEN WITH CULTURAL AND POLITICAL BAGGAGE

When I say "climate change," what do you hear? Some hear scientific consensus and the need for a carbon price. Others hear more government, extreme environmentalists, restrictions on freedom or the free market, and even a challenge to their notion of God. These are their real concerns, and they may all be triggered by this one term. The science of climate change represents a transformative shift in our sense of who we are and how we are connected to the natural world. It is to be expected that such a cataclysmic shift in cultural beliefs would be met with fierce resistance from those who are invested in the status quo for ideological, political, or economic reasons.

To understand the processes by which people make sense of climate change, we must understand that people's opinions on this and other complex issues are based on their prior ideological preferences, personal experience, and values—all of which are heavily influenced by their referent groups and their individual psychology.[10] Physical scientists may set the parameters for understanding the technical aspects of the climate debate, and business people may offer solutions, but both have a lot of work to do in influencing whether society accepts or even understands their conclusions. The processes by which people understand and assess climate change go far beyond its technical merits. Their reasoning process is suffused with emotion that sets boundaries to reach a predetermined end that fits their cultural worldviews. When people hear others talk about climate change, they may, for example, feel an implicit criticism that their lifestyle is the cause of the issue or that they are morally deficient for not recognizing it.

The key to engaging people in a consensus-driven debate about climate change is to engage the emotionality of the issue and then address the deeper ideological values that may be threatened to create this emotionality. The upshot is that scientists and business executives (both present and future) need to evolve in both their understanding of science and their ability to communicate it if they wish to lead their organizations in the challenges of the twenty-first century. If business schools do not include some coverage of communication skills to balance an increase in science content in the business curriculum, they will have left a gaping hole in the education of future business leaders. Successful and effective management requires an ability to clearly communicate an idea and mobilize people to address it. There is a heavy emphasis in business education on developing the "right" strategy. In the world of business, that is not enough; there needs to be greater attention directed toward how to turn that strategy into successful practice.

CHAPTER 10

# WORLDVIEWS AND
# SOCIAL MOVEMENTS

IN THE 2016 PRESIDENTIAL ELECTION, climate change became
as big a wedge issue as abortion, with 85 percent of conservative Republicans questioning the science and 79 percent of liberal Democrats accepting
it.[1] Research has examined several factors that explain this divide. For example, studies have shown that people whose values are relatively hierarchical
and individualistic are more likely to be skeptical of climate change, as such
a belief would necessitate controls on industry and commerce, a future that
many—particularly conservatives—do not desire. People whose values are
more egalitarian and communitarian tend to support the notion of climate
change, as solutions are consistent with a distrust of commerce and industry
as being damaging to society and worthy of regulation and control, a future
that many—particularly liberals—support.[2] Similarly, studies show a strong
correlation between support for free-market ideology and rejection of climate
science.[3] Other studies connect climate denial to a distrust of environmentalists and the belief that climate change is a left-leaning liberal issue. The ideological dimensions of this debate are many. But increasing commentary, both
partisan and nonpartisan, is making it clear that the conservative position of
denying climate change is becoming untenable.[4]

This is valuable knowledge for future business leaders, understanding the
deeper psychology and sociology of why people reject a conclusion that is endorsed by nearly two hundred scientific agencies around the world,[5] including

the scientific agencies of every one of the G8 countries.[6] And equally important is an ability to understand how social movements mobilize on one side or the other of such a conclusion, how those movements change, and what role corporations play in that movement. This can go a long in way in helping future business leaders anticipate market shifts around issues such as climate change and influence their development.

In the decade of the 2010s, the US has had a partisan divide over climate change, one that is starting to recede in the 2020s. Of the nine major conservative parties in such countries as Australia, Great Britain, Spain, and New Zealand, only the US GOP does not at least admit climate change is a problem.[7] As countries such as China and India step forward with climate plans of their own in order to develop energy and mobility grids that reflect climate controls that they see coming, supporting arguments for the social movement that resists climate policy begin to break down. That breakdown continues as the economics of renewable energy such as wind and solar reach price parity with fossil fuels.

And it breaks down even further as the voices expressing concern over this issue are expanding beyond constituents that skeptical Republicans don't trust—environmentalists, democratic politicians, and scientists—and including constituents they do trust—business executives, religious leaders, and fellow Republicans. The social movement and the politics around the issue are rapidly changing, and this is important for business leaders who wish either to take a passive stance and monitor political shifts that will lead to regulatory or market shifts or take a more aggressive stance to lead those shifts and create momentum for addressing this critical economic threat.[8]

## SOCIAL MOVEMENTS SHIFTING AROUND CLIMATE CHANGE

There are many domains in which to see how the voices on climate change are shifting.

First, key business interests are taking public stands on the need to address climate change when faced with projections like those from Moody's Analytics that estimated that damage from climate change could cost the United States between $54 trillion and $69 trillion by 2100.[9] Similarly, Mark Carney, when governor of the Bank of England, warned that if we do not take action now, global warming could become one of the biggest risks to future economic stability[10] as increasingly severe "events damage infrastructure and private property, negatively affect health, decrease productivity and destroy wealth."[11] Where business leaders were previously reticent to step into highly contentious political debates such as this one, they are now having a hard time staying silent as continued inaction threatens their economic future. Cargill executive director Greg Page has warned that climate change is real and must be addressed to prevent future food shortages that could "impact the potential for us to feed the 9 billion people that we could be confronting [by 2050]."[12] General Mills CEO Ken Powell told the Associated Press, "We think that human-caused greenhouse gas causes climate change and climate volatility and that's going to stress the agricultural supply chain, which is very important to us."[13]

These are not isolated voices. They represent a growing concern within the corporate sector that we have a problem and government inaction will only make it worse. Because these messages are not coming from the traditional voices that have been sounding the alarm bell from the environmental community—the Environmental Protection Agency, the United Nations Intergovernmental Panel on Climate Change, Al Gore, or an environmental nongovernmental organization—they carry a weight with skeptical constituencies that will find their message more readily persuasive.

Second, religion has entered the fray. Notably, the Pope has stepped forward to say that climate change is real and that we should do something about it as a matter of religious morality. In his encyclical letter *Laudato Si* and his speeches to the Joint Sessions of Congress and the United Nations, he broke the link that says you cannot believe in God and believe in climate change, as some have claimed. Whereas Rush Limbaugh devoted an entire episode of his show to make the argument that climate change and a belief in God are mutually exclusive,[14] the Pope argued that the idea that the book of Genesis grants us "dominion over the earth" "is not a correct interpretation of the Bible as understood by the Church" and that its persistence "has encouraged the unbridled exploitation of nature by painting [man] as domineering and destructive by nature." This led him to prominently warn world leaders that "[w]e need to act decisively to put an end to all emissions of greenhouse gases by mid-century at the very latest, and to do even more than that."[15] The Pope's message was followed by similar statements from prominent Muslim,[16] Jewish,[17] and Buddhist[18] leaders. Muslim clerics from twenty countries, for example, signed the Islamic Declaration on Climate Change in 2012, calling on Muslims and all nations worldwide to address climate change, and two hundred rabbis and cantors from all the Jewish denominations and movements joined with the Coalition on the Environment in Jewish Life, Shomrei Breishit, and the

Jewish Council on Public Affairs to issue a joint declaration in support of the Pope's encyclical letter.

Third, Republicans are hearing it from fellow Republicans. In 2015, fifteen Republicans joined thirty-five Democrats in voting for an amendment that affirmed that humans contribute to global warming. Later that year, eleven House Republicans signed a resolution that recognized humans have a role in causing climate change and endorsed steps to address it.[19] Former governor George Pataki (R-NY) and Senator Lindsey Graham (R-SC) have added their voices to those of other Republicans who are now trying to convince their party to agree with scientists—as have key supporters of President Trump such as Representative Matt Gaetz (R-FL), who in 2019 broke with the president and said that "we can believe the climate deniers or we can believe our eyes."[20] New proposals are emerging to create a "Manhattan Project" for clean energy funding to encourage nuclear energy, hydropower, and "carbon capture" technology.[21] Representative Greg Walden (R-OR), the ranking member of the House Energy and Commerce Committee, called for increased funding for nuclear power "which is safe, reliable and emissions free, and which experts agree must be part of our strategy to reduce emissions," and Representative Dan Crenshaw (R-TX) called for funding of carbon capture and storage technology that he said can "clean up the environment, promote innovation."[22]

To keep the momentum going, Jay Faison, a conservative Republican businessman, spent $10 million on efforts to lobby skeptical Republicans to embrace the issue of climate change.[23] Former Congressman Bob Inglis (R-GA) has made it his mission to get his party to see the scientific facts (and won the 2015 Profile in Courage award from the John F. Kennedy Library in the process). Conservative think tank R Street, started by former Heartland Institute staffer Eli Lehrer, is actively searching for conservative methods for addressing the issue.[24] The conservative business lobbying group American Legislative Exchange Council (ALEC) has begun to shift its position. Though Shell, Google, and other corporations quit the group because its positions on climate change are incompatible with their own,[25] ALEC not only insists that it doesn't deny climate change but has threatened to sue those who suggest otherwise.[26] Even the United States Chamber of Commerce, which historically has lobbied against regulations to curb emissions, issued a press release in 2019 promoting the "pioneering groundbreaking solutions" in the energy sector to curb climate change.[27]

Finally, it appears that Republican voters are changing. Public opinion polls by *Bloomberg*,[28] the Pew Research Center,[29] Yale University,[30] and Clear-Path[31] show that Republican voters are becoming believers. By 2015, the majority of Republicans—including 54 percent of self-described conservative Republicans—had come to believe that the world's climate is changing and that mankind plays some role in the change. This is a marked change from 2009, when just 35 percent of Republicans believed that climate change was real, and the trend line is on a steady upward slope.

Surveys by the Yale Program on Climate Change Communication showed a fourteen-point jump in belief in climate change among Americans between 2015 and 2018.[32] More significantly, this included a fourteen-point jump between 2017 and 2018 among liberal to moderate Republicans who think global warming is happening (68 percent) with 55 percent thinking it is mostly caused by humans. When asked why they are changing their position, their answer referenced first the recent extreme weather events we have witnessed (such as hurricanes in Florida and Texas, and more localized anomalies such as unusually heavy rains, droughts, floods, and temperature swings) and second the increasingly convincing arguments by people and groups they trust that this is real. And these surveys were conducted before the devastating California wildfires in 2018, which killed over a hundred people and caused up to $400 billion in damages, making them the most expensive natural disaster in US history.[33]

All of these shifts are suggestive that the tide is turning and that climate change policy and a resultant market shift are increasingly likely. By analyzing the social movements around this issue, business leaders can see that momentum is building. Yet while more people are changing their opinion to match the overwhelming majority of scientists, there are some skeptics who can never back down. Senator James Inhofe (R-OK), for example, has staked far too much of his rhetoric, reputation, and theatrics (such as throwing a snowball on the Senate floor) on the belief that climate change is "the greatest hoax ever perpetrated on the American public." And talk show hosts such as Rush Limbaugh and entire organizations such as the Heartland Institute have left themselves little room to make a face-saving change. Instead, one should expect their voices to get louder as their numbers decrease.

The question for business leaders then becomes, when will the firmly entrenched inertia against climate policy break? President Trump's denial of the issue and the influence of the fossil-fuel lobby have led congressional Republicans to be reticent to go against the party.[34] But many Republican politicians, congressional aides, lobbyists, and staff believe in the science and the need to take action when safely behind closed doors. They are just waiting for the right political cover to come out in public with their views. Jerry Taylor, president of the Niskanen Center, has had unusual access to Republican politicians as a former staff director at ALEC and vice president of the Cato Institute and states, "I have talked to many of them in confidence. There are between 40 and 50 in the House and maybe 10 to 12 in the Senate. They're all looking for a way out of the denialist penitentiary they've been put into by the Tea Party. But they're not sure what the Republican response ought to look like exactly and when the political window is going to open."[35] Will the voter base really take out their wrath if they acknowledge the science? That day may have passed, as some have begun to speculate that the climate denial movement is losing its momentum and falling into disarray.[36] In fact, many Republican voters may now be willing to reward a candidate who expresses a belief in science[37] and avoids what former presidential candidate Jon Huntsman warned against in 2011: the Republican Party becoming the "anti-science party."[38]

Business leaders must watch, and if possible influence, this debate. The importance for society to address climate change cannot be understated, on both moral and economic grounds. While business leaders have a personal stake in the former, they have authority and expertise to speak about the latter. In fact, in December 2019, seventy-five CEOs whose companies employ more than two million people signed a letter alongside union leaders who represent 12.5 million workers to urge that the US maintain its commitment to the Paris Climate Agreement.[39] Business leadership can shift the tide on issues like climate change, changing them from strictly environmental issues to becoming seen as economic issues that affect all sectors of the market and could have dire implications in the future if left unchecked. When the issue is put into those terms, business has no choice but to engage the public debate to influence the future direction of their markets. Business students need know-how to play that role with increasing frequency in the future.

# CHAPTER 11

# THE RADICAL FLANK AND
# THE CLIMATE CHANGE DEBATE

"We need to view the fossil-fuel industry in a new light. It has become a rogue industry, reckless like no other force on Earth. It is Public Enemy Number One to the survival of our planetary civilization."

WITH THESE WORDS in *Rolling Stone* magazine in 2012, environmental activist Bill McKibben launched a radical and moral broadside against the fossil-fuel industry and its contributions to climate change.[1] In a coordinated move, the McKibben-founded climate advocacy group 350.org launched its Go Fossil Free: Divest from Fossil Fuels! campaign with a stated goal to "revoke the social license of the fossil fuel industry." With the help of activist college students, the movement sought to stigmatize fossil-fuel companies, restrict future cash flows, and depress share prices by compelling universities to divest their holdings in these companies.

The effort seems to some to have been a failure, at least by the financial measures that were laid out.[2] Only a limited number of institutions have divested their endowments, and the stocks of major fossil-fuel companies show little effect. But in doing a network text analysis of news articles, Todd Schifeling of Temple University and I found that by other measures the effort has been a success.[3] Exhibiting a phenomenon in the social sciences called the "radical flank effect," McKibben and 350.org have dramatically altered the climate change debate in the United States by expanding its scope, reorienting its center, and injecting new ideas and concepts to help focus the true depth of the issue. Their success on this dimension offers important insights for business leaders to understand critical dynamics of the broad ecology of political, social, and market shifts and how they may play a role in their development.[4]

## ORIGINS IN THE CIVIL RIGHTS MOVEMENT

The radical flank effect was first introduced by sociologist Herbert Haines in 1984,[5] when he studied the civil rights movement of the 1960s. What he saw was that when Martin Luther King Jr. first began speaking his message of racial equality, it was perceived as too radical for the majority of white America. But Malcolm X entered the debate and extended the radical flank by rejecting white America and its Christian values, and preaching the supremacy of blacks over whites. As a result, his message made King's message of nonviolent direct action and passive resistance look moderate by comparison.

The effect of the radical flank on more moderate activists in the same cause can be either positive or negative. The negative radical flank effect creates a backlash from opposing groups. In such cases, all members of a movement—both moderate and radical—are viewed with the same critical lens. For example, some may think that all environmental groups should be judged by the tactics of those who spike trees to prevent logging or ram whaling ships. Conversely, the positive radical flank effect is when members of a social movement are viewed in contrast to each other; extreme actions from some members can shift the spectrum of the debate and therefore its center and make other organizations seem more palatable or reasonable.

Russell Train, second administrator of the EPA, articulated the positive radical flank effect in the 1970s when he quipped, "Thank God for David Brower. He makes it so easy for the rest of us to be reasonable."[6] Brower, the first executive director of the Sierra Club, was a controversial figure who pushed the environmental movement to take more aggressive actions by taking strong stands (included running a controversial full-page advertisement on the back of the *New York Times* calling for wide-scale opposition to a dam in the Grand Canyon) and founding increasingly radical groups.[7] Brower once said, "The Sierra Club made the Nature Conservancy look reasonable. I founded Friends of the Earth to make the Sierra Club look reasonable. Then I founded Earth Island Institute to make Friends of the Earth look reasonable. Earth First! now makes us look reasonable. We're still waiting for someone else to come along and make Earth First! look reasonable."[8]

## THE RADICAL FLANK EFFECT AND DIVESTMENT

It was in 2012 that McKibben and 350.org staked the radical flank by mobilizing students to pressure their colleges and universities to liquidate their investments in fossil-fuel companies. This was a far more extreme position than was previously taken by activists in the climate change debate. That is, where others argued for industrywide controls on carbon without demonizing any particular industry, McKibben's radical flank portrayed the fossil-fuel industry as a public enemy and called for its extermination. The campaign's goal was to stigmatize—and thereby harm—the market value of fossil-fuel companies.

But we found that the ultimate effect of their efforts was not so much financial as on the terms of the debate over climate change. By using text analytics software to sift through forty-two thousand news articles about climate change between 2011 and 2015 and map the influence of the radical flank, we found that the divestment campaign expanded rapidly as a topic in worldwide media. In the process, it disrupted what had become a polarized debate and reframed the conflict by redrawing moral lines around acceptable behavior.[9]

The evidence suggested that this shift enabled previously marginal policy ideas such as a carbon tax and carbon budget to gain greater traction and more widespread use in the debate. It also helped translate McKibben's radical position into new issues such as "stranded assets" and "unburnable carbon," the idea that existing fossil-fuel resources should remain in the ground. Although these latter concepts are still radical in implication, they adopt the language of financial analysis and began appearing in business journals such as *The Economist*, *Fortune*, and *Bloomberg*, which made them more legitimate within business circles. Thus the battle cry of divestment became a call for prudent attention to financial risk. By being addressed in these financial publications, the carriers of the message shifted from grassroots activists to investors, insurance companies, and even the governor of the Bank of England.[10]

In the end, about 150 college campuses worldwide had committed to fossil-fuel divestment as of 2018, including 50 in the United States; over 600 US schools signed the American College and University President's Climate Commitment; and a survey at Harvard in 2017 found 67 percent of faculty favored divestment, with 9 percent opposed and 24 percent neutral.[11] 350.org reports that assets committed to divestment have leapt from $52 billion in 2014 to more than $11 trillion in 2019.[12]

These changes represent far more than shifts in invested capital. They represent and signal increasing shifts in the public debate and public awareness over climate change and its cause. Bill McKibben and 350.org have made actions that would have been considered unreasonable in 2011 commonplace in 2019. They have staked the radical flank and gained greater attention to the financial and business aspects of the debate and the role of investments in continuing the climate crisis. Although the divestment campaign chose an objective that was largely impossible to fulfill (that is, put the fossil-fuel industry out of business), its tactics expanded the boundaries of the public debate and enhanced the viability of progressive issues. Business students and business leaders should be made aware of these shifts, understand the science that is driving them, and develop strategies to either employ it or respond when others do.

CHAPTER 12

# A NEW DEMOGRAPHIC IN THE CLIMATE CHANGE DEBATE

ONE OF THE ENDURING CHALLENGES for the environmental move-
ment is that it is indeterminate; it has no obvious constituency.[1] In settling issues of labor relations, we have workers and union officials. In settling issues
of civil rights or gender equity, there are minority and female workers and national organizations set up to represent them. However, with the environment
there are no natural constituents or bearers. A high-quality environment tends
to be a public good, which when achieved cannot be denied to others, even
to those who resist environmental reforms. For many environmental issues,
those who act to protect the environment can expect to receive no personal
material benefits. In fact, those who oppose environmental reforms are easier
to identify, on the basis of threatened material or political interests.

For example, strong opposition to an acceptance of climate change science
has come from a very obvious source: industry groups, libertarian think tanks,
and Republican politicians who stand to lose economic or political power if
the science is accepted and actions to address it are taken. They have come
to be called the "climate change counter movement"[2] and seek to sow doubt
about the reality of climate change and challenge the legitimacy and integrity
of scientific institutions and analyses.

But recently a new movement has emerged whose interests are aligned with
climate action: young people. The Sunrise Movement and the Youth Climate
Strikes have created a new constituency that is changing the landscape of the

debate. We now have a specific and aggrieved party—young people—and a specific set of interests that is under threat—their future. And they have a powerful and charismatic spokesperson in Greta Thunberg, who has galvanized attention on their concerns and was chosen as *Time* magazine's 2019 "Person of the Year."[3] This combination of factors creates a powerful force for mobilizing for action.

Indeed, a Yale University study found that the members of the current college-age generation (eighteen- to twenty-two-year-olds) "have grown up with more exposure to the effects of global warming than their parents and grandparents. Perhaps it isn't surprising then that polls find young adults are particularly concerned about global warming."[4] The report also found that "millennial Republicans are more likely to say global warming is happening, is human-caused, and that most scientists agree it is happening, and they are more likely to worry about global warming than older Republicans." A 2019 survey by Glocalites found that even the number of young Republican voters aged eighteen to thirty-four who are worried about the issue rose by 18 percentage points from the prior year to 67 percent.[5]

And this movement also creates a sympathetic foil for those who are trying to decide where they stand on the issue. These young people have parents, uncles, aunts, and grandparents, all of whom can be empathetic to their plight and call for action. And research shows that children are having an effect on inspiring adults toward greater levels of climate concern.[6] After all, the research showed that parents really do care about what their children think.

And we also have politicians who can see this demographic as voters who are raising their voices. Governor Jay Inslee (D-WA) had a great deal to do with the attention to climate change in the 2019 Democratic Debates, and the youth movement had a tremendous influence in keeping it there. Thousands of young environmental activists, calling for the Democratic Party to embrace far-reaching plans to curb climate change, gathered outside Detroit's Fox Theater during the July 2019 Democratic Debates and were quite vocal in pushing for a climate crisis town hall in September 2019. This is all in marked difference to the 2016 presidential debates, in which the climate change issue was largely ignored.

Finally, these young people are future employees, and companies took notice and took action. In the September 2019 climate strike, almost fifteen hundred workers at Amazon's headquarters in Seattle walked out of work, as did employees at Facebook and Google. Further, the strikes were joined by some faculty unions, Britain's Trades Union Congress, and many others.

All in all, these young people are lending their voices to an increasingly vocal public debate over climate change. According to surveys by Yale University, between 2013 and 2018, the percentage of people who are alarmed or concerned by climate change rose from 45 percent to 59 percent, while those who are doubtful or dismissive dropped from 27 percent to 18 percent.[7] Where previous years' surveys showed a steady and unchanging 25 percent who will speak about the issue with family or friends, the 2018 Yale University survey found that number rising to 33 percent.

Once more, evidence makes it clear that business students and business leaders should become more conversant in the scientific and political aspects of public debates that will eventually (likely sooner rather than later) create shifts within the market to which corporations will have to respond, and in many cases, companies will want to respond. Importantly, these young people are tomorrow's business leaders, voters, consumers, and investors, and the education they need must reflect the world they will inherit and enter. As thoughtful and engaged leaders, they will see the opportunity to contribute to solving a problem that is being made clearer and more urgent every day by a host of constituencies and concerns. It is past time to respond.

# PART 4

# BEING AUTHENTIC

# CHAPTER 13

# BUILD A LOW-CARBON WORLD FROM A HIGH-CARBON LIFESTYLE

SOMETIMES IT SEEMS LIKE no business executive can support action on climate change without being labeled a hypocrite. This would appear to apply across the political spectrum. When Google hosted a conference on addressing global temperature rise in August 2019, Fox News ran a piece headlined, "Google summit on climate change attended by stars in private jets, mega yachts slammed as 'hypocritical.'"[1] Several months earlier, the left-leaning site ThinkProgress had published a story titled, "The Stunning Hypocrisy of JP Morgan and CEO Jamie Dimon on Climate Change."[2]

In both cases there was some truth to the critiques. The $20 million Google event was attended by celebrities and leaders who arrived in 114 private jets—not a great look for a summit aimed at reducing humankind's carbon footprint. And though JP Morgan's Dimon has talked about the urgency of fixing climate change, his bank has provided nearly $200 billion in financing for fossil fuels since the 2015 Paris climate treaty was signed.

But it's also the case that the charge of "hypocrite" tends to get made against anyone who speaks out publicly about the defining existential issue of our time. "Since we all somehow use fossil fuels and carbon-free replacements are still the exception (for now), charges of hypocrisy would have to apply to pretty much all of us," Amy Harder argued in *Axios*.[3]

Now certainly, those who care about climate change need not live in caves and wear hair shirts before their message is taken seriously. But if climate change is so serious and we intend to address it in our professional lives, why are we not at least trying to change our personal lives? As we consider this next step of merging our personal and professional selves to address issues that we are in part causing, we need to do it without judging others, without judging ourselves, and with a clear awareness that individual action alone will not create the kinds of changes in technology, culture, and behavior that will be at a scale necessary to address this global problem. There are no easy answers, but our business schools should be teaching the next generation of leaders how to work through these complex questions.[4]

### DON'T JUDGE OTHERS

We are all human, with our own ambitions and foibles, strengths and weaknesses, opportunities and constraints. And we all develop justifications for the decisions we make. We might tell ourselves that our individual actions don't matter and that it is up to governments to solve the climate change problem. Or we may tell ourselves that we need to fly, eat meat, or turn on the air conditioner; we're not hurting anyone; everyone else does it; other people are far worse. We all have ways of developing self-serving narratives. No one is immune, especially when we don't know how to easily live carbon-free lives.

Some use the analogy of addiction to describe our high-carbon lifestyles, arguing that we are addicted to oil, travel, or consumption and can't stop. But this analogy is perceived as judgmental at its core and can make people defensive or self-righteous. The issue becomes "us versus them," as some people virtuously think of themselves as "healthy" for living a low-carbon lifestyle and others feel criticized for having the "illness" of addiction. I have heard people having to defend their choice of turning on an air-conditioner, driving a large car, or eating meat. That is not the way to change our society. We are all in this together, and none of us really knows what a fully carbon-free lifestyle looks like. In a sense, we are all addicts with the same malady, and there are no healthy people we can look to in order to gauge normal behavior.[5] There is no room for judgment here. In fact, I've found that some of the most self-righteous people on the issue of the environment tend to draw the line between acceptable and unacceptable lifestyles right where they reside, usually in a scale for Western lifestyles. They signal their virtue by driving an electric car, purchasing renewable energy credits, flying less, and eating less (or no meat). Might someone from India (with 1.1 metric tons of $CO_2$ emissions per person per year) or Kenya (with 0.3 metric tons) agree that any Western lifestyle is a sustainable one, when the average American releases nearly 20 metric tons?[6] Where is the line of virtue?

Instead of dividing people on environmental issues like climate change, what we need are leaders who have a vision for where we need to go as a society, can model behavior that gets us there, and display empathy for those who are unsure about following. That role falls to all of us, and especially those who graduate from business schools because they will possess a degree of power to change the economic, political, and cultural systems that others will not.

### DON'T JUDGE OURSELVES

Just as blaming others for the problem of climate change is not productive, the same is true for self-blame. We must not fall into the trap of feeling inadequate or a fraud on the basis of an expectation of purity. There are serious limitations to taking individual action on climate change, and we can't allow the perfect to be the enemy of the good.

Climate change represents a challenge different from other environmental issues such as litter or killing a member of an endangered species. These are discrete choices, whereas virtually every lifestyle activity (and virtually every manufacturing activity) entails the creation of some degree of greenhouse gases, whether it's heating one's home or driving to visit family. The simple truth is that, as Canadian environmental activist David Suzuki points out, "We don't have the infrastructure to be ecologically neutral." But he continues,

> Right now, the important thing is to share ideas and change minds, and the way I do that is by meeting with people or speaking. Unfortunately, in Canada, that means I have to fly, and flying generates a lot of greenhouse gases. Still, it doesn't mean that we don't need to try to minimize our ecological footprint. I did that by trying not to use a car, or when I needed to, I bought the first Prius sold in Canada. We have a rule in our household: if you're going to work or school, you take a bus or walk. We've reduced our garbage output to about one green bag a month, and I think we can reduce it further. But every time I jump in a plane, it negates everything else I do to live sustainably. . . . [We need to acknowledge] that these things matter. We have to at least try because we're hoping to convince others that they all have to try, too. But there are different levels of contribution each person can make.[7]

And that is the key: each of us has to begin the effort in a way that fits our knowledge, circumstances, convictions, and possibilities. We must each start where we are and learn to become aware of our impact, the ways those impacts may be reduced or eliminated, and the challenges with taking action.

## TAKE INDIVIDUAL ACTION

Start slow and start realistic. Real and lasting change has to be gradual and careful. Big grand changes, just like big grand New Year's resolutions, have a tendency to fail. Take that first step, but not with the goal of changing the world. Instead, start your personal journey with no idea where it will take you.

Begin by educating yourself. Try a personal carbon calculator. Learn about your direct and indirect emissions and where they come from. Read a book or perhaps take a class. Second, explore ways to reduce those impacts in ways that fit your lifestyle demands. Go to any one of the many Going Green Checklists for countless ways to get started, or the EPA's webpage on what you can do to address climate change. Insulate your home, screw in an LED light bulb, recycle your toilet paper roll, change your investment portfolio, change your career, volunteer for an environmental group, buy a programmable thermostat, buy a more fuel-efficient car, buy a bicycle, don't buy anything at all, and think about what you consume! Try giving up meat. If not permanently, try it for a short time, perhaps for Lent (if you are very ambitious, try giving up carbon for Lent).[8] After all options are exhausted, learn about purchasing carbon offsets to support projects in communities across the country that reduce greenhouse gas (GHG) emissions beyond what you can achieve through individual action.

## ECO-BENEFITS OF STAYING HOME

One activity that has garnered considerable attention for behavior change among my academic colleagues is to stop flying to conferences.[9] One study found that transportation accounts for 75 percent of the carbon footprint of a PhD student and attending conferences accounts for 35 percent of that carbon footprint.[10]

In response, Kevin Anderson, professor of energy and climate change at the University of Manchester, took a train to a conference in China, convinced that this added to the legitimacy of his science. Professor Laurie Zoloth, who directs Northwestern's Center for Bioethics, Science and Society, calls upon scholars to take a sabbatical from academic conference travel every seven years to allow the Earth to rest. In October 2015, a group of fifty-six scholars from more than a dozen countries launched a petition calling upon universities and academic professional organizations to greatly reduce their flying-related footprints as part of the effort to limit the destabilization of the climate system.[11] A 2019 study by UBS found that 16 percent of British travelers and 24 percent of US travelers are allowing climate change concerns to cut the number of flights they take. As a result, the study concluded, the annual growth in US flights would fall from the expected 2.1 percent to just 1.3 percent and the growth rate in EU flights would be cut in half, leading to a reduction in revenues for Airbus of roughly $3 million.[12]

While this may be the answer for some, it may not be for others. For example, colleagues at some smaller colleges need conferences to make connections and gain access to the latest research. In the end, conferences are an important aspect of what researchers do for a living and simply stopping them seems, in my opinion, counterproductive. Instead, be mindful of which conferences you go to and how; lobby conference organizers to eliminate paper programs, water bottles, or the serving of meat; or use web conferencing when practicable. Consider the carbon footprint of your lifestyle in its totality before deciding where to act.

But in the end, we should not lose sight of what we do best. Researchers do good research and share it with others. Business executives operate their organizations to serve a market, earn a profit, provide jobs, and serve society. Beyond that, all of us can speak out on climate change, use our knowledge to vote for politicians who propose action on the issue, and recognize that we need to also change the system.

### HOW TO CHANGE THE SYSTEM

But let's be honest with ourselves; individual actions alone will not solve the problem. They will give us insights on the solutions and a sense of the magnitude of change that is necessary to change our culture of values and behavior. But the necessary changes must come from a shift in societal norms and market rules. It will require a challenge to the dominant notions of consumerism, shifts in the rules of capitalism, and a reexamination of the role of the corporation in society.

If designed properly, policies that address climate change will reduce or even eliminate the impact of individual behavior. For example, Dr. Grischa Perino from the University of East Anglia's Centre for Behavioral and Experiment Social Science offered a provocative argument that green consumers who voluntarily choose *not* to take a flight *within* the EU for environmental reasons will, in fact, have "no impact on total emissions" because the EU Emissions Trading System requires that any additional emissions from flights be fully offset (where, paradoxically, bus travel emissions are not).[13] While some criticize the result as being too theoretical and not reflective of the implementation realities, this is what regulations are supposed to do: change the entire system, not just pieces of it. And the thoughtful individual needs to develop a deeper understanding of the environmental implications of simple actions.

Such understanding should also consider the political and social implications, as some see something sinister in the focus on individual action. Author Murray Bookchin warned that "it is inaccurate and unfair to coerce people into believing that they are personally responsible for present-day ecological disasters because they consume too much or proliferate too readily. . . . If 'simple living' and militant recycling are the main solutions to the environmental crisis, the crisis will certainly continue and intensify."[14]

### CULTURE AND BEHAVIOR CHANGE INVOLVES US ALL

In the end, the challenge of climate change, indeed the broader challenge of living in the Anthropocene, requires a broad-scale shift in our culture. This shift must take place from the bottom up and the top down. Those of us who care about climate change must model a way, if not solely by action, at the very least by the effort of trying. We need to practice the art of being mindful, thinking and behaving differently than the dominant cultural norms of consumption tell us to think and behave. We must strive to both advocate and embody a new worldview, one that moves from carbon constrained to carbon neutral to eventually carbon negative. Or, as scholar John Ehrenfeld describes it, shifting from being less unsustainable to being more sustainable.[15] None of us knows how to do this yet.

But as Pope Francis pointed out in his 2015 encyclical letter *Laudato Si*, any effort in the right direction, "however small it may be, opens us to much greater horizons of understanding and personal fulfillment . . . [and] a greater sense of responsibility, a strong sense of community, a readiness to protect others, a spirit of creativity and a deep love for the land." He goes on, "There is a nobility in the duty to care for creation through little daily actions. . . . We must not think that these efforts are not going to change the world. They benefit society, often unbeknown to us, for they call forth a goodness which, albeit unseen, inevitably tends to spread. Furthermore, such actions can restore our sense of self-esteem; they can enable us to live more fully and to feel that life on earth is worthwhile."[16]

This is the essence of individual action, to strive for a new awareness and model behavior that others will respect, admire, and emulate. We should do this not for external validation, but as a means to act with integrity and authenticity. We can't explore this new reality in the abstract. We have to strive for change at the larger scale while also experimenting with changes in our own everyday lifestyles. True authenticity resides in both.

# CHAPTER 14

# BRIDGE SOCIAL DIVISIONS

**WHILE WE STRIVE** to become authentic, addressing the great challenges of our day by making changes in our personal lives, we must also develop the skills to communicate the need for change with others. Many business executives are stretching the boundaries on that task. In fact, we are in the midst of a profound shift in how business leaders participate in the public sphere. It used to be that executives actively avoided weighing in on contentious political or social issues. The conventional wisdom was that it was always better to stay out of the spotlight. Choosing sides on something like police violence, inequality, immigration, or gender could hurt sales and revenues or draw you into a public relations controversy outside of your control.

But today, executives are facing pressure to speak out for their customers, their employees, and even fellow business leaders. "Political and social upheaval has provoked frustration and outrage, inspiring business leaders like Tim Cook of Apple, Howard Schultz of Starbucks, and Marc Benioff of Salesforce—among many others—to passionately advocate for a range of causes," read an article by business professors Aaron Chatterji at Duke and Mike Toffel at Harvard on the growing wave of CEO activism, adding, "The more CEOs speak up on social and political issues, the more they will be expected to do so. . . . In the Twitter age, silence is more conspicuous—and more consequential."[1]

The risks of speaking out publicly are still very real for businesses— Starbucks faced a boycott from conservative consumers after criticizing the

Trump administration's Muslim ban in 2017. Yet not taking a stand on a contentious issue can also cause damage—Uber faced a liberal boycott, for example, because many customers felt the ride-sharing company wasn't active enough against the ban. *Bloomberg* sums up this tension by saying the CEOs are forced to walk a tightrope in "boycott culture."[2]

There are signs that the partisan tensions in this political climate are not going anywhere soon, and executives will increasingly be forced to become public figures on a range of issues. That is why our business curriculum needs to be preparing students with social and political science literacy for the divisive culture and fractured market environment they are entering.

The truth is that the market system that raised the standard of living for millions of people over the course of centuries is now, in the words of economist and Nobel Laureate Joseph Stiglitz, in need of being "saved from itself."[3] Former Unilever CEO Paul Polman now called capitalism "a damaged ideology" that "needs to be reinvented for the 21st century."[4] These are not isolated warnings, and all of them center on two unprecedented and systemic problems that capitalism is both causing and presently unable to address: income inequality and climate change. Darren Walker, president of the Ford Foundation, warns that these problems threaten our democratic values, discourse, and institutions.[5] Ray Dalio, founder of Bridgewater Associates, the world's biggest hedge fund, called income inequality an "existential threat" to capitalism, which he labeled a broken system,[6] warning that we could face increased populism, conflict, and "revolution of one sort or another" if it is not fixed.[7] Marc Benioff, CEO of Salesforce, warned that "we can no longer wash our hands of our responsibility for what people do with our products . . . it's time for a new capitalism—a more fair, equal and sustainable capitalism that actually works for everyone and where businesses, including tech companies, don't just take from society but truly give back and have a positive impact."[8]

So the next time you're at a Thanksgiving or holiday dinner, or any other event where you'll be forced to interact with people with different viewpoints and from different political backgrounds, think about how to weigh in on these issues. Begin with concern about the state of capitalism and move into climate change and income inequality in a way that creates consensus. Think of it as a test run for the types of challenges that business leaders face in the public arena. Instead of avoiding that unpleasantness, it may be a time to embrace it.[9]

## PERIOD OF FLUX

There is an opportunity for change before us right now. Yale University survey data from 2019 show that "over the past five years, the proportion of Americans who think global warming is happening and who worry about it has increased sharply. During this time, Americans have become increasingly convinced that global warming is happening (+11 percentage points), is human-caused (+15), and that most scientists agree it is happening (+15)."[10] And just as important, people are speaking up about it.

A shift is under way and can be propelled forward by conversations. This is how social change happens—in fits and spurts—something I've studied in looking at how culture shapes public debates around environmental issues. American physicist and historian Thomas Kuhn first described this process as moving between periods of stability and periods of chaos. In the former, one set of beliefs dominates other beliefs as the "paradigm."[11] But periods of flux begin when tumultuous events upset this paradigm and a chaotic search for a new paradigm begins. Borrowing a term from evolutionary biology, social scientists call this process of rapid social change "punctuated equilibrium."[12] The key is to push for change when things are most chaotic. Any executive knows that it is easiest to push for change when things are at their worst. As Winston Churchill advised, "Never let a good crisis go to waste." Try thinking about that over your Thanksgiving dinner.

## LIVING IN WORLDS OF OUR OWN DESIGN

Our country has broken into deeply divided tribes: left versus right, urban versus rural, the coasts versus the middle.[13] A 2014 Pew Research Center survey found that political polarization has markedly increased since 1994, with a doubling of both the overall share of Americans who express consistently conservative or consistently liberal opinions (from 10 percent to 21 percent) and the share that hold negative views of the opposing party (27 percent of Democrats and 36 percent of Republicans), even believing the opposing party's policies "are so misguided that they threaten the nation's well-being."[14] We have become suspicious of each other, questioning motives before considering ideas. Facts, it seems, have become less important than the political and ideological affiliation of their source. We seem to consider evidence only when it is presented by those who represent our tribe, and we dismiss information that is advocated by sources that represent groups whose values we reject.

This divide is ever deeper today because of social media. Social media has "democratized knowledge" because the gatekeepers for determining the quality of information have been taken down. But social media also creates the conditions for what has been termed fake news to run rampant.[15] Web-based media sites, and increasingly social media services such as Twitter, Facebook, and LinkedIn, allow us to find information to support any position we seek to hold and find a community of people that will share those positions—a phenomenon known as confirmation bias.[16] As a result, the internet doesn't always make us more informed, but it often makes us more certain. We self-create what Eli Pariser calls our "filter bubbles."[17] And this has the potential to radicalize entire

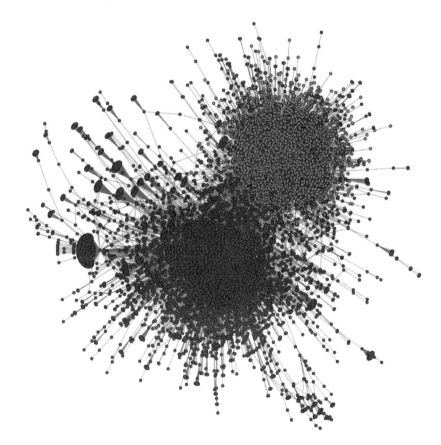

FIGURE 7   The Political Retweet Network. Notes: Laid out using a force-directed algorithm. Node shading reflects cluster assignments. The lighter cluster is made of 93 percent right-leaning users, while the darker cluster is made of 80 percent left-leaning users. Source: M. Conover, J. Ratkiewicz, M. Francisco, B. Gonçalves, F. Menczer, and A. Flammini, "Political polarization on Twitter," *Proceedings of the Fifth International AAAI Conference on Weblogs and Social Media*, 2011, 89-96. © 2020 Association for the Advancement of Artificial Intelligence (www.aaai.org), used with permission.

countries, as we saw in the way that YouTube helped make it possible for the far-right politician Jair Bolsonaro to become president of Brazil.[18]

In one vivid illustration of this phenomenon, a research study of two hundred and fifty thousand tweets during the six weeks leading up to the 2010 US congressional midterm elections found that liberal and conservative populations primarily retweeted only politically similar tweets. As shown in Figure 7, the researchers used a combination of network clustering algorithms and manually-annotated data to depict the network of political retweets as exhibiting a highly segregated partisan structure, with little interaction between the left- and right-leaning users.

### TO ENGAGE IS NOT TO ACQUIESCE

A 2016 study by the Pew Research Center found that "49% of Republicans say they're outright afraid of the Democratic Party, with 55% of Democrats saying they fear the GOP."[19] This part of the cultural divide is self-reinforcing: we fear the other so we don't engage; we don't engage so we fear the other even more. To break this loop, we need to do what columnist Thomas Friedman calls "principled engagement."[20] We need to reach out; listen to opposing viewpoints; ground debate on solid research, data, and facts; and seek ways to find common ground. While some may choose to sit on the sidelines or hope that one side or the other fails, there is too much at stake.

But some can choose to build bridges, recognizing that the mere act of engagement does not mean an acceptance, an endorsement, or even that we like the other side. It is merely a recognition that we have common concerns and interests. Standing in the middle of warring tribes is not easy, as it invites attacks from both sides. But someone has to try by finding common ground. A 2017 study by the Pew Research Center signals the urgency to bridge these warring tribes. As shown in Figure 8, the gap between the left and right has grown recently from a divide into a chasm, with decreasing engagement between the two.

### WHERE TO START THE CONVERSATION?

One place to start middle-ground conversations—whether at a Thanksgiving dinner or in the workplace—is with the economy and the extent to which it does, or does not, serve all equitably or whether it can address the climate change problem. While some do not believe that we have an income inequality problem,[21] the numbers are sobering, and they were made more vivid by the

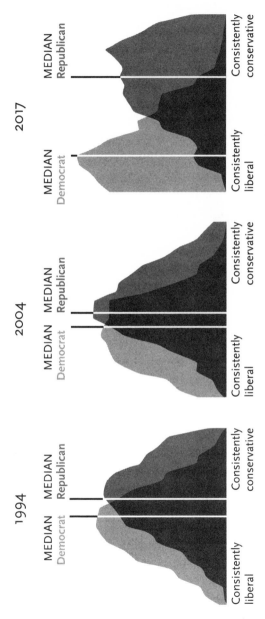

FIGURE 8 Democrats and Republicans More Ideologically Divided Than in the Past: Distribution of Democrats and Republicans on a Ten-Item Scale of Political Values. Notes: Ideological consistency based on a scale of ten political values questions. Survey conducted June 8–18, 2017. Source: M. Dimock, J. Kiley, S. Keeter, and C. Doherty, *Political polarization in the American public* (Washington, DC: Pew Research Center, 2017), used with permission.

COVID-19 crisis. More important, voters on both the left and right increasingly believe what they tell us.

Between 2009 and 2012, 91 percent of all income growth was enjoyed by the wealthiest 1 percent of Americans,[22] and they still pushed for more tax relief in the present administration. In 2018, nearly 20 percent of the Fortune 500 companies had an effective federal tax rate of 0 percent despite having made a profit.[23] That caps off a period when the share of income earned by the richest 1 percent of Americans increased from 10 percent of the total economic pie in 1979 to 20.1 percent in 2013.[24] A more startling imbalance in *assets* draws a picture that is even bleaker. In 2014, the top 1 percent of American households possessed 38.6 percent of the nation's wealth, while the bottom 50 percent possessed –0.1 percent.[25] Data suggest this will only get worse, as the problem is chronic. Of Americans born in 1940, 90 percent ended up richer than their parents. Of Americans born in 1980, only 50 percent are expected to do the same,[26] as the wage-quality of jobs steadily declines, with younger workers (aged eighteen through thirty-four) seeing the highest decline.[27] Today, the three wealthiest Americans have more wealth than the bottom 50 percent (one-fifth of Americans have zero or negative net worth).[28]

This is not just a problem within the United States. The World Inequality Report finds that "income inequality has increased in nearly all world regions in recent decades," marking "the end of a postwar egalitarian regime which took different forms in these regions," shown in Figure 9. Globally, the wealthiest 26 people in the world own as many assets as the poorest 3.8 billion people on the planet.[29] The World Economic Forum reported that "most economies are failing to provide the conditions in which their citizens can thrive, often by a large margin."[30]

Disparities like these are the source of concern that many American voters feel—a vein that both Republican Donald Trump and Democrat Bernie Sanders tapped into in the 2016 and 2020 presidential elections (along with Senator Elizabeth Warren in 2020). At its core, it represents a distrust of our political and economic institutions. Some direct their ire at government, some at the corporate sector, and many hold great disdain for the seemingly corrupt relationship between the two.

So what should you talk about to bridge this conversation? Well, to begin, if there is absolutely no hope of common ground, stay away from politics and talk about football. But is there an opportunity to build bridges by introducing topics of common concern to start the conversation and then focus on solid data

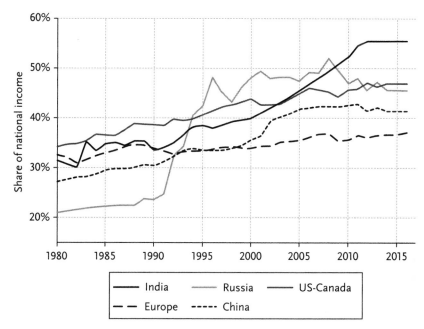

FIGURE 9  Top 10 Percent Income Shares Across the World, 1980–2016. Notes: See wir2018.wid.world/methodology.html for data series and notes. In 2016, 47 percent of national income was received by the top 10 percent in US-Canada, compared to 34 percent in 1980. Source: F. Alvaredo et al., *World inequality report* 2018 (World Inequality Database, 2018), used with permission.

and solutions? This is where business logic and insights can help. On inequality, there is an opportunity to talk about the corrupting influence of money in politics and possibilities for campaign finance reform; the practice of influence peddling and the proposal for time limitations on when government officials can become lobbyists; programs to increase opportunities for upward mobility, such as making college education more affordable; or programs to help ease the burden that workers feel when they are displaced by technology, automation, globalization, or policy shifts.

On climate change, there is an opportunity to point out that since 2008, the cost of solar energy has dropped more than 80 percent, wind energy dropped more than 50 percent, battery storage more than 70 percent, and LED lighting more than 90 percent. As a result, in the words of Hal Harvey, CEO of Energy Innovation, "a clean future now costs less than a dirty one."[31] It may not be easy or pleasant at first, but it's at least a start. And maybe you'll be surprised at the common ground you're able to find.

One positive outcome of our increasingly contested and hostile partisan political environment is that everyone seems to be engaged. Even though a large percentage of Americans didn't vote in the 2016 election, the 2018 mid-term elections saw a significant increase and the 2020 elections show even more. As more people enter the process, they need to find the right way to engage. Healing the country won't come from Washington. It will come from each of us at our family dinner tables, local Kiwanis Clubs, town halls, workplaces, and importantly, from our positions of power and influence as business leaders; that is, if you choose to use that power for the benefit of society. In my religious tradition, it is said, "blessed are the peacemakers." Whether or not you share my tradition, I think we can agree that we need more peacemakers. And while business schools are not generally designed to foster a peacemaker mindset, society would benefit if more collaborative leadership emerged from the business community to create consensus on the issues we face.

# CHAPTER 15

# CULTIVATE MULTIPLE WAYS OF KNOWING THE WORLD AROUND US

COMMUNICATING THE NEED to address the great challenges of our day and shifting our own lifestyles requires an awareness that there are multiple ways of knowing the world around us, of which analytical business thinking is but one. So the next time you find yourself, or hear others, preceding a statement with the line, "Speaking as a business person . . ." stop and reflect on all that is excluded with that one simple statement, and the extent to which it grants license to narrow one's focus. Corporate attorney James Gamble warned that "markets have for a great many people taken on the power to transform selfishness into a virtue." And importantly, that kind of thinking infects and spreads through our culture "so deeply we barely even recognize how much it guides our actions."[1]

Our lives cannot be run strictly by an objective of economic efficiency. Business executives are also human beings. You do not have to give up one to be the other. In fact, if you do, you will develop a blind spot for recognizing the full scope of the issues before us. Though the themes of this book are in contrast to author and commentator Anand Giridharadas's negative views on the role that business leaders can play in addressing our societal challenges, I agree with his view that "when [the market] becomes the only language, when it becomes the only way of thinking about the right thing to do, it leaves us with a very impoverished sense of how to live together. It's good for creating wealth and creating things and building things, but it's not a guide. It's not a useful vocabulary for living together."[2]

It is clear that some within business are interested in tackling large systemic problems like climate change. And this is a big change from even two decades ago when an executive choosing to pursue anything other than the accumulation of profits would have been rare. But when they do so, they usually put society's challenges into the language of the market. You hear about consumer demand for sustainability, the return on investment of renewable energy, or the business case for climate action. While it's positive that businesses are attempting to go beyond the false trade-offs between the economy and the environment, the challenges of our age require us to think larger than just in terms of the market.

Consider the present reality that geophysicists now argue we face, proposing that we have entered the Anthropocene, a new geologic epoch defined by humanity's influence on nature's systems. Many people respond to this crisis by looking to technology and consumer decisions as the solution—to more windmills, solar cells, or electric cars, and fewer plastic bags. According to this line of thinking, we have to change only a little about ourselves and instead just need better, more environmentally friendly gadgets. This narrow focus will lead us down an incomplete and ultimately wrong path.[3]

## MAKING OUR CHALLENGES TRIVIAL

Ecologist Aldo Leopold wrote in 1949, "No important change in ethics was ever accomplished without an internal change in our intellectual emphasis, loyalties, affections, and convictions. The proof that conservation has not yet touched these foundations of conduct lies in the fact that philosophy and religion have not yet heard of it. In our attempt to make conservation easy, we have made it trivial."[4]

His words bear repeating today. We have made issues like climate change trivial by making their solutions easy, looking for simple answers that are palatable, generally framing them in the language of commerce. We count carbon emissions and look to the decreasing price of solar cells and the increasing market value of Tesla as measures that we are making progress. But making the "business case" to address climate change is as absurd as making the business case to not commit suicide. And yet that is how we are trying to change our culture, one consumer transaction at a time.

In the long run, it won't work. While free-marketers and technology entrepreneurs may advertise otherwise, there are no technological or market-based silver bullets to solving our environmental problems. While they may reduce our carbon footprint, they will not make it go away. Electric cars are good but they are still cars that require energy and resources to be built, operated, recycled, and disposed of, all of which increase our carbon emissions (even if some of that energy comes from renewables). Geoengineering may be good as a way to ameliorate our impact on the environment (though many fear that it will make things worse). But both geoengineering and electric cars are designed to allow us to continue our prior lives without change—we will continue to live in ever-larger homes, drive ever-larger cars, and consume as we always have. In short, these are Band-Aid solutions that do not address the root problems that lie within our culture. While important in the short term, Elon Musk and the power of the market alone will not save us in the long term. In the long term, we will have to change the way we think.

## FINDING THE ULTIMATE SOLUTION IN
## OUR CULTURE AND VALUES

The source of the climate problem is not just our technology or economy. The source of the problem is our beliefs and the values that define their purpose and form. If we continue to desire perpetual economic expansion, endless population growth, more material stuff to buy and throw away, plastics in any form and purpose, and an environment that will never cease to provide the resources we want and accept the waste we dump into it, then we will fall back into the convenient and lazy mindset that technology and policy will fix the problem for us. But without systemic changes in our culture and values, we will never recover from the destructive path on which we are embarked.

Life in the Anthropocene is the ultimate "commons problem," in which our survival depends upon our collective actions and the morality of individual actions takes on new meaning. The fossil fuels burned for use in New York, Shanghai, or Moscow have import for the poor people in low-lying areas of Bangladesh and the coral reef ecosystems of Australia. The meat eaten on single-use plastic in Ann Arbor has an impact on the global environment we all share. We are all members of the same species that is threatened by the challenges of the Anthropocene. We are in this together. Therefore, there are times when we must describe our challenges in terms other than economic. This will open us up to solutions that will address the difficult challenges and choices that are required.

But how do we bring such thinking into our deepest values of purpose and meaning? Pricing undesirable products out of the market and shifting the market to innovate new ways to live our lives are helpful. But ultimately, we have to connect concern for the environment with our deepest sense of what we love and what we hold as sacred. We need to bring the human into our economic, social, and political thinking. Moving beyond the business case, we might ask, as author Duane Elgin does, "When will humanity express its moral outrage that it is wrong to devastate an entire planet for countless generations to come, just to satisfy the consumer desires of a fraction of humanity for a single lifetime?"[5]

Indeed, the world's wealthiest 20 percent consume 86 percent of all the world's goods and services while the poorest 20 percent consume just 1.3 percent.[6] This unprecedented and widening income gap is being paralleled by a similarly widening "climate divide"[7] in which the poorest of the world are least responsible for climate change and are most at risk, while the affluent of the world are most to blame but have the resources to adapt to its impacts. People in New York may be able to afford to build sea walls; people in Bangladesh may not. Consider as an example the recent trend in private firefighting teams in California after the Camp Fire to protect the affluent, their expensive homes, and their cautious insurance providers.[8] This is the market "solving" this problem. But it is a mirage. We allow the problem to continue but isolate the wealthy from its effects in the short term. In the long term, we all lose. That is a future reality that can only be solved when we frame the problem in terms of values that go far beyond dollars and cents.

By asking about the fairness and justice of the skewed distributions of the climate divide, we can begin to regain the language that it is simply the right thing to do to protect the global climate. The language of economics and commerce may be expedient, but it is incomplete; by using it, something is lost. Changing our actions to save money will only get us so far. Changing them because it connects to our deepest values of what is just, wise, and true can take us much further.

### MOVING BEYOND TECHNOCRATIC THINKING

Science and the market are important tools for understanding and addressing our challenges, but they are not the only ones. There are questions that quantitative and technocratic thinking alone cannot answer, but philosophy, theology, the humanities, and the social sciences, as well as tacit, vernacular, and pragmatic knowledge can help. What is life; what is beauty; what is love; what is right and just; how much is enough and sufficient to make us happy and fulfilled? These questions reside in the domain of what makes life worth living, and all are difficult terrain for quantitative, logical science.[9]

As David Brooks explained, there are layers of life that are covered by the rational science of economics, political science, and evolutionary psychology. "But those layers don't explain Chartres Cathedral or 'Ode to Joy'; they don't explain Nelson Mandela in jail, Abraham Lincoln in the war room, or a mother holding her baby. They don't explain the fierceness and fullness of love, as we all experience it." He went on to point out that love and "the passions are not the opposite of reason; they are the foundation of reason and often contain a wisdom the analytical brain can't reach."[10]

For example, science and economic thinking may lead us to see the value of a forest in terms of its market value as lumber or a carbon sink. But that means that it will only be protected until a higher economic or material value is found. Such reasoning, though logical, ignores the many values of the ecosystem that is a forest, which includes the complex array of life forms within it and their intricate interconnections and dependencies. It also ignores any deeper meaning and purpose that may be inherent or derived. So the simple act of cutting down a forest and replanting it with acres of corn, wheat, barley, or even more trees is not equivalent; it destroys the ecosystem and, as essayist Wendell Berry repeatedly reminds us, a piece of ourselves and our culture.[11]

This does not suggest a rejection of the scientific method, but a rejection of a purely technocratic approach and the excessive belief in the reductive power of scientific knowledge to pursue an ongoing conquest of nature. At its most extreme, it is a rejection of "scientism," the belief in the physical sciences to the exclusion of other forms of knowledge.[12] With its preference for quantitative over qualitative measures; focus on parts over the whole; and pursuit of outcomes such as human utility, technical efficiency, and political expedience as unquestioned goods, we are now learning to recognize that there are limits to a purely scientific understanding of how nature works and what we are doing to it. Though the development of new technologies to reduce our environmental impact is a good thing, they are only reducing the velocity at which we are running toward a brick wall; they are not changing course. As a metaphor, consider that we have ended the war in Iraq, but that is fundamentally different from creating the peace.[13] Stopping the war on nature that we now follow will not create the peace.

### THE IMPORTANT ROLE OF CHANGING OUR CULTURE

The climate challenge before us requires that we change our collective understanding of who we are as humans, how we come to understand the natural world around us, how we structure the social and economic worlds in which we operate, and how all three of those sets of values fit together. We won't create a socially equitable or environmentally sustainable world because of a set of data or economic self-interest. We will take these steps because we connect concern for the environment and our fellow human beings with our deepest sense of what we love and what we hold as sacred. To do this, we should be turning to religion and philosophy as a way to augment the market in making this shift.

If the collective responsibility we need in the face of today's social and environmental challenges is connected to the teachings of the Bible, Torah, Quran, Bhagavad-gītā, Tripitaka, and oral traditions of indigenous peoples, or the philosophies of Aurelius, Locke, Voltaire, Madison, Wordsworth, Thoreau, and Russell, then the world can change on its axis. When people hear the message from the church, mosque, synagogue, or temple to address climate change and protect the environment, it connects to their deepest sense of who they are and why they are alive. It connects, as social psychologist Jonathan Haidt explains, with their intuitive sense of morality, the values they share with the groups to which they identify, the sense of altruistic care they offer to what they love and the history that made all of this so.[14]

So while science and the market can continue to advance in exploring the rational in our world, by analyzing environmental and social systems through "big data" and economic modeling, they must also leave room for the subjective and all-too-human aspects of structuring our norms and beliefs. We must acknowledge the awe we may feel at nature's wonder, exercising a humility that recognizes we do not know its full complexities. We must also acknowledge a profound sense of responsibility that we may have for caring about the plight of those around the world (and within our own communities) as they struggle to survive in a local context that lacks clear water and proper sanitation or is being ravaged by the effects of climate change. Logic and reason seek to explain all phenomena through words and numbers. And yet there are many experiences that defy articulation: classical pianists or professional athletes often have great difficulty verbalizing the essence of their experience when they are perfecting their craft. There is much in the world that business logic can blind us from seeing. The protection of the natural world or the creation of a fair and equitable society must be a matter of judgment and a sense of what is right, not just what makes money.

### ENVISIONING A BETTER FUTURE

In an address at Rice University in 1962, President John F. Kennedy challenged the nation to go to the moon. "We choose to go to the moon in this decade and do the other things, not because they are easy, but because they are hard, because that goal will serve to organize and measure the best of our energies and skills, because that challenge is one that we are willing to accept, one we are unwilling to postpone, and one which we intend to win, and the others, too."[15] This decision was not made on the basis of economic calculations. In fact, many at the time were not sure it could be done, as the task required an enormous advance in the science of flight in a very short period of time. Manned space-flights were only three years old at the time, and scientists had barely begun to set their sights on the moon when President Kennedy issued his challenge.[16]

In the same way, we must now set our sights on presently unattainable goals, looking to solutions that economics and the market may now say are impossible, but will one day solve. We must make an inspirational challenge like President Kennedy's to be a net positive influence on the environment by moving from carbon reductions to carbon neutral to even carbon negative and providing nutrition for the ten billion people who will inhabit the planet by 2050. These are the kinds of goals that market thinking may blind us from seeing, much less trying to achieve. But just as we rose to the challenge of putting a human on the moon, we can achieve these goals if we set our sights on achieving them.

As we look ahead, many futures are possible, and we will not know how much we have changed for centuries to come. But that is the point. These challenges represent a marathon, not a sprint. Solving them will transpire over the course of our lives as well as those of our children and grandchildren, in time periods far longer than the next quarterly return, the next innovation cycle, or the vesting of your pension plan. Without facing up to this level of depth and this length of time, we will overlook the scale of the challenge, and many will give up far too soon. To address the full scale of these issues, we must transcend the language of the market and strive for the aspirational that will give us hope that we can solve our problems.

And this is an area in which business can lead. Many students come to business schools with this goal in mind, to leave a mark on society that makes it better than when they found it. Business education can cultivate such noble motives within its graduates and encourage future leaders to see themselves in the longer arc of history, not just the tenure of their next step up the career ladder. By thinking of a legacy now, business students can ensure that they guide their careers with higher aspirations in mind, aspirations that seek to serve society through the power of commerce.

The words that President Kennedy used at American University in 1963 to discuss the challenge of creating peace in the world can be applied to our environmental and social challenges today: "Too many of us think it is impossible. Too many think it unreal. But that is a dangerous, defeatist belief. It leads to the conclusion that war is inevitable—that mankind [sic] is doomed—that we are gripped by forces we cannot control. We need not accept that view. Our problems are manmade—therefore, they can be solved by man. And man can be as big as he wants. No problem of human destiny is beyond human beings. Man's reason and spirit have often solved the seemingly unsolvable—and we believe they can do it again."[17]

# PART 5

# ENVISIONING YOUR CAREER IN MANAGEMENT AS A CALLING

# CHAPTER 16

# THE FUTURE WORLD

HOW WILL THE WORLD be different in the future, and what role will you want to have in making it a world you want to see? This is a question I want every business student and business leader to ask themselves. A freshman in my class today was born around 1998 and will (statistically) die around 2078. The next generation of freshman born today will live into the twenty-second century. How will the world be different as they reach the end of their years? The answer, of course, is impossible to define. But we know for certain that the future will be different in ways that are unimaginable.

Consider the example of my grandmother, Christina Johanna Hoffman, who was born in 1899 and died in 1995 (see Figure 10). In the course of her lifetime, she witnessed the advent of indoor plumbing and home electrification, the Wright Brothers' first flight, the debut of the Ford Model T, and humans landing on the moon, just to name a few. If I had told her about the future when she was in her twenties, she would not have believed me. So too will it be for our students today and the world they will grow old to experience. The changes they will see are just as incomprehensible today as flight or space travel would have been to my grandmother when she was young.

But that doesn't mean we can't speculate and imagine what life will be like in the next fifty to seventy-five years. As just one example among many, there will be spectacular change in the personal automobile as it morphs into personal mobility. This change will not just be technological; it will also be

FIGURE 10 Christina Johanna Schneider (1899–1995). Married Joseph Leo Hoffman (1898–1967) on September 29, 1921.

economic, political, and, above all, cultural. How we think about *mobility* in the future will be completely different from how we think about *owning and driving* a car today.[1]

## AUTONOMOUS, ELECTRIC

As a first step in this imagination exercise, two assumptions are in order. First, improvements in battery storage technology will make electric cars practical for large swaths of the American public in the next fifty to seventy-five years, particularly in urban and suburban settings. This is a view shared by most within the automobile sector and appears within reach, as the 2019 Chevrolet Bolt and Tesla Model 3 both promise a range of two hundred to three hundred miles at a cost of just over $35,000. Second, the driverless car will be further developed and in widespread use in the same time frame, again particularly in urban and suburban centers. Though some recent projections are bit more skeptical of a rapid rollout,[2] let's imagine this longer-term rollout, given the amount of research and development[3] and rapid advancements[4] that are being devoted to this challenge. With those two assumptions, let's allow our imaginations to run.

A future form of mobility may mean that, rather than relying on a human driver, you will use your phone (or some new form of communication device) to summon a driverless car to pick you up and take you where you need to go, whereupon you will release the car to transport someone else to their destination. You will choose your driverless car provider by convenience, and that will depend on how well the provider's network connectivity algorithms are designed for efficiency and speed. Just like the airline business model, mobility providers will make more money when their cars spend as little time idle as possible. This means that they need to anticipate demand. We may expect to become more impatient and therefore more demanding with mobility providers, expecting wait times to be shorter and shorter.

Presumably, these driverless cars will be safer,[5] having fewer accidents, fewer drunk drivers, and fewer thefts (though it will still happen, fewer people will steal a car that is fully integrated and tracked in a network). In 2018, the National Highway Traffic Safety Administration released the results of crash tests for the Tesla Model 3, and the car earned five stars in every category;[6] many expect computers to be safer drivers than humans (for one thing, they are not distracted by texting while driving). These factors suggest that highway speed limits may rise as car safety improves and human error is taken out of the equation. This may also mean that anyone who chooses to drive in a driverless era will pay more for insurance, thus creating even more pressure for fewer people to own cars.

Those that continue to own cars will have to find ways to easily access electricity, leading to the need for new social norms and new technologies for buying electrons. For example, we may drive three hundred miles to visit friends. But will those friends still be excited to see us if they are asked to pay for the electricity to fill up our vehicle?

Awkward moments aside, there will always be people who prefer to enjoy the pleasure of driving or are afraid to get into a driverless car. Certainly we would not expect driverless motorcycles even as they become electric (Harley Davidson released its electric motorcycle, the Live Wire, in 2019). But eventually we should expect to see more acceptance of driverless cars as the fears of them subside. Remember that automatic elevators were introduced in 1900 and, though they were safer than manually operated elevators, people were so afraid of them that it took over fifty years to convince the public that they were actually safe to the point that they could start designing most buildings to include them.[7] The transition to self-driving cars could be much faster. Indeed, no less than Bob Lutz, the legendary auto executive, has stated, "It saddens me to say it, but we are approaching the end of the automotive era."[8]

We may eventually see a day when most people will no longer desire to own cars. This idea, called the "peak car" hypothesis, is hotly debated in automotive and academic circles.[9] But we can already see signs of this trend in today's young people[10] and urban dwellers,[11] neither of whom wants the hassle of owning, parking, insuring, or just worrying about a car. When I tell students in my class that I love cars, they look at me like I have three heads. In fact, many young people show little interest in even possessing a driver's license. The emergence of companies like Uber, Lyft, Maven, and Zipcar is a sign that the sharing economy is displacing car ownership as the rite of passage that it once was.

### COMPUTERS ON WHEELS

The emergence of driverless car services leads to the question of how many cars there will be on the road in the future. Right now, the average car is parked 95 percent of the time.[12] If we move to a full model of "mobility on de-mand," there will be fewer cars on the road, since these vehicles will be shared. So we would just need enough cars for peak demand; imagine somewhere around 50 percent to 70 percent fewer cars on the road in a perfectly efficient mobility system. While this may worry parts suppliers, some manufacturers speculate that the number of passenger miles will stay the same even as the number of cars decreases, yielding a stable market for parts such as tires, shocks, and brakes.

Where does that take us? First, the average homeowner will no longer need that garage out back, or even the driveway that accesses it, leading to a growth in conversions to apartments or storage. Contractors will like this development. We can also expect a growth in new urbanism, or walkable cities designed for pedestrians and bike riders rather than car habitat, since many urban roads and parking garages will no longer be needed and must be repurposed. City planners will like this challenge.

Where will these remaining cars be housed and fueled? Well, they can go idle wherever they are best positioned for the morning's demand after finding the nearest connection to an electricity source for refueling. This could spell the end of the neighborhood gas station, a long fixture on the American landscape. For one thing, gasoline will no longer be necessary. For another, corporate mobility providers will build their own charging stations. This could spell trouble for oil-producing nations,[13] as the more than 50 percent of the oil that is used for vehicle travel will no longer be needed.

Who will make these cars and what will the market look like? On this question, chairman of the Rocky Mountain Institute Amory Lovins offers an interesting provocation. In his view, the car of the future is not a car with a computer; it is a computer on wheels.[14] As such, it is not necessarily the incumbent car companies that can make it. It could also be made by electronics and computer companies. This is a trend we are already seeing, as Apple, Google, and others enter the car market. One key to their product offerings is the emphasis on new software to add to the hardware we all know. Indeed, we can expect the big nameplate automobile companies to make the transition to the mobility providers from whom we rent rather than buy. The moves by GM to invest in Lyft and Sidecar foretell this emerging trend. Or, some wonder if the traditional automotive companies will become merely hardware suppliers—what insiders call "contract metal-benders"—to Apple, Foxconn, and Google automotive.

This marriage of mobility providers and car manufacturers will lead to a different set of design parameters for the car of the future. While there will still be a demand for status symbol vehicles, people will choose mobility more for interior comfort and efficiency in getting from point A to B than for exterior styling.

So where does that leave those of us who still like that exterior styling? More specifically, where does that leave the classic and vintage car market?[15] First, we can expect to see the number of auto aficionados dwindle, as young people no longer share a love affair with cars. This could lead to a drop in demand, just as we've seen a drop in demand for record albums, and therefore a drop in prices for the classic cars we love today (though I have seen vintage record albums commanding some pretty high prices, as people seem to be returning to them in certain specialty markets).[16]

So just as there are those who hang on to their old turntables in lieu of CDs or MP3s, and still ride horses despite their long ago displacement by the automobile, there will be those who will hang onto their classics. These people will have to make special arrangements to keep their garage and find ways to store a supply of gasoline (which they may buy from a specialty store). These owners will also have to rely increasingly on their own repair skills or a specialized service market as the decline of the neighborhood gas station takes with it the neighborhood car repair shop. This may lead to an increase in classic car storage clubs, complete with private service facilities. This is happening already; M1 Concourse is a private car facility in Troy, Michigan, where an exclusive community of more than two hundred and fifty secure private garages is set alongside a 1.5 mile private motor speedway.[17]

### LOST JOBS

Might we see some strange or problematic scenarios in the electric, driverless world of the future? Certainly. Many have already called out the privacy and security issues and what would happen if someone hacked into the driverless car networks.

But going further, might driverless cars actually increase congestion? Imagine a scenario in which someone goes to dinner in the city and knows that demand will be high for cars when it is time to leave. Might that person choose to "instruct" a personal car, or a hired car, to continuously circle the block until they are ready to leave, thus leading to increased congestion as well as competition for rides? Or imagine being able to sleep while commuting to work; might this encourage increased sprawl and suburbanization as people choose to live farther and farther from work? There are also many people (disabled, aged, and children) for whom personal mobility is not easily accessible, but a future of on-demand, autonomous vehicles could allow them this benefit. Could the result be a net increase in the number of cars on the road, at least in urban centers?

Or is there a problem waiting to happen with the preprogrammed algorithms that these cars will possess for making decisions in emergency situations? What will happen when a car faces a "choice" between a bad and worse outcome, say between hitting a pedestrian and a motorcycle or school bus (which is also driverless and likely communicating with the car)? The legal ramifications of such a "decision" are not hard to imagine and have already been tested, when an Uber self-driving car killed a pedestrian in 2018 (though the company settled a civil case with the pedestrian's family, prosecutors decided not to file criminal charges against Uber[18]).

Finally, as has been true since the beginning of time, technological innovation displaces some jobs while it creates new ones. Already, we might anticipate the demise of the taxi driver, gas station owner, or mechanic. But driverless car proponents also look to end the careers of long-haul truckers, as this is one of the first targets of the technology.[19]

And what will this transition mean for public transportation or for lower-income communities? Will buses, subways, and trains take a hit because more people of means choose their driverless private pods? Will people in the developing world be able to access this technology and, if not, will the availability of new "old-fashioned" automobiles begin to dwindle? Will the continuous maintenance of older cars be the norm, as has happened in Cuba, where it is not an uncommon sight to see a perfectly maintained 1957 Chevrolet driving down the street? If this is the future, will driverless cars increase economic inequality in the country and the world?

## DON'T JUST ENVISION YOUR FUTURE, CREATE IT

Of course, all of this is speculation. But while it is fun to imagine what might be, the future will be what we make it. As Abraham Lincoln said, "[T]he best way to predict your future is to create it." That is the message I leave with my students after I introduce them to my late grandmother. And that is the message I would like to leave with you. While we can imagine the world you will see later in your life, the better exercise is to ask you what kind of world you want to see and what role you want to play in bringing it to reality.

# CHAPTER 17

# YOUR ROLE IN YOUR OWN FUTURE

LET'S CLOSE WITH the provocation offered in the previous chapter. What kind of a future do you imagine, and what role do you want to play in making it a future you want to see? How will you use your career in management to make it so? These are the questions of this book, and the answer it proposes is that you find a calling within management, one that is designed to serve not just shareholders but also society—employees, customers, the community, the natural environment. In the end, if these interests are not included in business decision making, then society will be doomed. Our economy, and increasingly our politics, will be driven by selfish short-term greed, seeing value only in shareholder value and profits and neglecting the deeper values of why we work, why we live, and what kind of a world we wish to leave for our children and grandchildren.

We need more business leaders who want to assume the responsibility that comes with the great power they possess by using that power to improve the world for all of us, not just a select few. David Brooks described this focus as a shift from résumé virtues to eulogy virtues in setting goals for your life.

The résumé virtues are the skills you bring to the marketplace. The eulogy virtues are the ones that are talked about at your funeral—whether you were kind, brave, honest or faithful. Were you capable of deep love? We all know that the eulogy virtues are more important than the résumé ones.

But our culture and our educational systems spend more time teaching the skills and strategies you need for career success than the qualities you need to radiate that sort of inner light. Many of us are clearer on how to build an external career than on how to build inner character.[1]

Can we foster that shift earlier in life rather than waiting until one reaches their fifties or faces some kind of crisis that knocks them off the path of self-oriented goals of status, affirmation, and achievement? This is particularly important for those in business, as their actions have an impact not only on their own careers but also on the lives of those who must live with their decisions. People in business have a tremendous and increasing influence on how our society is structured, whether that is through the resources they control, the political clout they wield in government, the ability they have to sway public opinion, or simply the salaries they derive—between 2017 and 2018, CEO compensation grew at double the pace of ordinary workers' wages, rising to a median of \$18.6 million after a median raise of \$1.1 million, or 6.3 percent, from the year prior.[2]

In short, corporations play an outsized role in our modern world. As professors of organizations, Dick Scott at Stanford University and Jerry Davis at the University of Michigan write, "Their presence affects—some would insist that the proper term is *infects*—virtually every sector of contemporary social life."[3] The actions of corporations, as much as the individuals who inhabit them, decide how we will live and adapt in a world that climate change, species extinction, income inequality, and other social and environmental issues are altering. Corporations can, at their best, "be vehicles of social progress and the solution to basic problems such as the provision of food, healthcare, education and other human needs and wants" and, at their worst, "provide the tools to multiply the effects of the darkest of human impulses and result in terrorism, genocide, and labor camps."[4]

Unfortunately, business education has not kept pace with the challenge of creating business leaders who will serve the world. In his book *From Higher Aims to Hired Hands*, business professor Rakesh Khurana at Harvard warned that, though business schools were "originally founded to train a professional class of managers in the mold of doctors and lawyers to seek the higher aims of commerce in service to society," the modern business school format has "effectively retreated from that goal, leaving a gaping moral hole at the center of business education and therefore, management itself."[5] He argued that "business schools have largely capitulated in the battle for professionalism and have become merely purveyors of a product, the MBA, with students treated as consumers. Professional and moral ideals that once animated and inspired business schools have been conquered by a perspective that managers are merely agents of shareholders, beholden only to the cause of share profits." It is time, he concluded, "to rejuvenate the intellectual and moral training of future business leaders." That is one of the objectives of this book, to trigger the process of rejuvenating the intellectual and moral training of future business leaders, whether that is through institutional changes in business school curriculum or individual changes in how business students approach their studies.

So my questions and challenges for you, the present or future business manager, are, How will you rejuvenate your intellectual and moral training to be a future business leader? How will you use the power that you will or already possess? What kind of a legacy do you want to leave? What do you want your eulogy to say? What kind of a future do you want to help create?

## THE MANY POSSIBLE FUTURES BEFORE US

Dev Jennings of the University of Alberta and I have written about possible future realities in the face of the Anthropocene and a world faced with deepening environmental problems and widening inequality. Humans are causing these problems and, therefore, humans can solve them. But, the solutions must be as systemic as the problems we have created, and they must rest on the political and economic institutions of our society, not only on technology. In considering how we may create one future or another, we have to consider how our beliefs must change on the basis of questions such as, Who has a voice in articulating our challenges and potential solutions?, What values do these people and groups bring to bear for explaining our problems?, and How does the process of problem definition lead to the types of solutions we create? A problem defined is more than half solved, so the answer to these questions sets the trajectory for what our future world will look like.

The COVID-19 crisis was a test of our institutions and offered a glimpse into what the future may hold for how we will respond to climate change and the crossing of other planetary boundaries. The global community faced a collective crisis, one that required that we work together to address a problem that we had created. We discovered that some institutions were inadequate and in need of rebuilding while others worked. The response from certain sectors of the federal and global government, for example, were less than what many would have wished for. But other institutions at the state, local, economic, and nonprofit regimes mobilized as a collective response. We witnessed many self-less responses that focused on the collective good from health care workers, scientific institutions, postal workers, corporations, and religious institutions, all issuing a call for shared responsibility and community relationships. If we are to respond to the "new normal" of the Anthropocene, a world with increased storm severity, droughts, wildfires, and the movement of vector-borne diseases, we will need to strengthen the collective institutions and values uncovered by COVID-19 and address the individualistic institutions that lead to denial and competition. Whether we are successful in that effort will determine our fate.[6] In preparation for what is coming in the Anthropocene, will we develop more resilient social, technological, and economic systems, or will we maintain the status quo, deny that a "new normal" is upon us, and lock into a structure of institutions that are ill-equipped to handle the problems that we are soon to face? Will we work together for the common good or will we compete for finite resources? With considerations like these, we can begin to envision multiple possible futures that lie along a spectrum ranging from the dystopian to the utopian.[7] These possible futures are not separate and distinct; each will reveal itself in our world. Indeed, all of them are visible now to one degree or another. The question for future leaders is which future will you strive to make the dominant one? The future is ours to create, based on the choices we make today.

## Collapsing Systems

On the dystopian end of the spectrum, no one actor or movement emerges to define the problems we face or the solutions that address them, and we continue to bicker as they worsen. Our public and political discourse become animated by disagreement over not only the reality of our emerging Anthropocene problems, but also the social, political, and scientific institutions on which that understanding is based. While certain groups will continue to speak to the challenges we face—such as the United Nations, World Bank, and National Academies of Science—their voices will be unable to deliver knowledge with certainty or authority and are blunted by other actors offering contrary assessments, such as the fossil-fuel and electric utility industries. Multiple, divergent, and competing perspectives will lead to little consensus or consideration for solutions such that we continue down the path of political and economic polarization, yielding social strife and perhaps even violent revolt. Critical events such as increased hurricane, wildfire, or drought conditions or the threat of complete water loss in cities such as Cape Town, Bogata, and Sao Paulo will be framed as "normal" variations requiring no special forms of response.

Over time, this future will lead to ever-increasing government dysfunction, market failures, and social incivility, which will limit our ability to enjoy many of the benefits that we take for granted today. Roy Scranton, an author of many books and articles on the Anthropocene, warns of a collapse in culture that parallels that resulting from past genocides. He asks whether "we will be able to transition to a new way of life in the world we've made, one where we can no longer take many things for granted, such as: a global marketplace capable of swiftly satisfying a plethora of human desires; easy travel over vast distances; air-conditioned environments; wilderness preserved for human appreciation; better lives for our children; safety from natural disasters; and abundant clean water."[8]

We can see elements of this possible future in today's world. We see people and organizations who deny the reality of climate change and COVID-19, ignore warnings and regulations for behavior change, and take actions focused on individual survival or even personal and monetary gain at the expense of the collective well-being. Debate is hyper-polarized, as people and organizations retreat into their "tribes" to challenge the conclusions of scientific institutions when they threaten their entrenched beliefs. Amplifying this confusion and distorting the debate are social media channels such as Google, Facebook, and Twitter that introduce an increasingly diverse range of viewpoints, opinions, and "facts" of varying degrees of legitimacy, labeling uncomfortable realities as "fake news," delegitimizing experts by equating their research to mere opinion, and increasing the hyper-polarization of perspectives and worldviews that make any kind of meaningful dialogue or debate fruitless, if not impossible.

For those who wish to preserve their position within the economy and continue behavior and thought as before, this allows maintenance of the status quo, but only temporarily as collapses in social and environmental systems make the status quo untenable due to either massive economic disruption from increasingly damaging storm events or social disruption in the form of mass political mobilization in protests, the voting booth, or violence. In his book *The Uninhabitable Earth*, journalist David Wallace-Wells warns of such a dystopian future, but also notes that there is great uncertainty in predicting that future because it is unclear what humans will do to change it.[9]

## Market Rules

In this intermediate scenario, which is presently the most likely, corporate interests dominate discourse and the institutions and values of the market prevail. Any effort to address our environmental or social problems will be taken for monetary reasons. In fact, economic value will overrule most other values. We will make the "business case" to address climate change and ban certain products only if more lucrative products are found. The environment will continue to be treated as an economic asset, valuable only for the resources it provides to humankind. Motivations for protecting the environment would be based on the extent to which they create jobs, increase market activity, or satisfy other logics of business strategy. The overarching goal of continuous economic growth would remain sacrosanct, with the environment seen merely as an economic input, one leveraged with innovation and technology to create growth. A forest, for example, will be seen only as an economic asset, either as a source for commercial lumber or as a carbon sink. Any attempts to protect such an asset for values other than economic will be limited, particularly if they restrict human development through job loss or stranded assets.

Many of the market failures that caused our social and environmental problems will be maintained, as certain groups benefit from the political and economic institutions as presently arranged. The logics and values of this scenario will be a mere expansion of prior concepts of corporate environmental concern that are based on maximizing eco-efficiency, seeking to reduce environmental impact by pursuing profit maximization. An attendant belief is that the market will always yield socially positive outcomes and market success would eventually lead to environmental or social remediation. Environmental crises like hurricanes, droughts, and floods will be viewed as either "normal" weather events, if solutions involve any form of restraint on the market, or business opportunities if markets exist for solving them.

Unfortunately, many metrics of the market agenda, such as gross domestic product (GDP), return on investment (ROI), and discount rates, do not capture the full scope of environmental or social impact and act as limited guideposts for recognizing, much less solving, the problems we face. In all of these cases, money and the time value of money are all that register and the associated environmental and social costs are overlooked. Companies providing new climate-saving products such as electric cars (such as Tesla) and rooftop solar arrays (such as Solar City) will enjoy greater success, as they produce goods and services that allow consumers to continue to consume as they always have. In this scenario, the government itself is a supporting actor for the market, creating regulations that perpetuate economic growth. Though it may not be captured completely, it negotiates outcomes for the benefit of the market. For example, Greg Shill, professor of law at the University of Iowa, has argued that American public policy throughout the twentieth century "enforced dependency on the automobile . . . to conform to the interests of Big Oil, the auto barons, and the car-loving 1 percenters of the Roaring Twenties."[10]

For those who want to pursue a solution to our social and environmental problems using presently dominant logics and values, this scenario will appear to be the most expedient way forward. Trajectories of some environmental problems may be reversed to the extent that efforts to address them maintain economic growth and corporate competitiveness. The Montreal Protocol, for example, was successful in restricting the production and sale of ozone-depleting CFCs only after DuPont developed a commercially viable alternative refrigerant.[11] The term "rules" in this scenario is a double entendre, referring both to the rules of the market logic defining the future and the extent to which the market rules over all aspects of life (both human and nonhuman). Such a future reality will remain unstable and dynamic, not necessarily because environmental and social problems create pressures for change, but because consumer interests shift and evolve.[12]

## Re-Enlightenment

On the utopian end of the spectrum, we witness a future in which the values of all members of society reflect both acceptance of the realities of our systemic social and environmental challenges and changes in the way our social, political, and economic institutions are configured. This scenario will involve a deep cultural transition akin to the Enlightenment of the seventeenth and eighteenth centuries. While the term "Enlightenment" carries some cultural baggage (not the least of which is whether the period accelerated colonialism and exploitation), the comparison is useful for capturing the scale and scope of the culture shift before us.

Prior to the Enlightenment, people in European regions were embedded in a set of "Middle Ages" institutions that shaped their view of society and nature: nature was unknowable, animated by mystical forces, and subsumed human society. But after the Enlightenment, we exalted human ability to dominate nature and ushered in the "Age of Reason," in which the natural world came to be viewed as a machine that could be dismantled, dissected, and reassembled to achieve human desires. The present transition from the Enlightenment to Re-Enlightenment suggests a similar recasting of our social institutions and the creation of new ones. From a Middle Ages worldview in which nature determined human society, to an Enlightenment worldview in which society determined nature, we now find ourselves faced with an Anthropocene worldview in which society and nature are interconnected, mutually and simultaneously determining one another.

Neil Evernden, professor of environmental studies at York University, captured the scale of this shift in his 1993 book, *The Natural Alien*, when he wrote, "The [environmental] crisis is not simply something we can examine and resolve. We are the environmental crisis. The crisis is a visible manifestation of our very being, like territory revealing the self at its center. The environmental crisis is inherent in everything we believe and do; it is inherent in the context of our lives."[13] In 2014, Rory Rowan, post-doctoral fellow in political geography at the University of Zurich, continued this thinking when he wrote, "The Anthropocene is not a problem for which there can be a solution. Rather, it names an emergent set of geo-social conditions that already fundamentally structure the horizon of human existence. It is thus not a new factor that can be accommodated within existing conceptual frameworks, including those within which policy is developed, but signals a profound shift in the human relation to the planet that questions the very foundations of these frameworks themselves."[14]

In fact, we may be seeing early signs of the emergence of this scenario as we witness the introduction of sustainability concerns within the realms of religion and philosophy. Pope Francis's encyclical letter *Laudato Si*, which sought to bring ecological considerations into Catholic social teaching, was accompanied by similar statements from the Jewish, Muslim, Hindu, and Buddhist faiths to call attention to our modern cultural ailments of rampant consumerism, unrestrained faith in technology, blind pursuit of profits, political shortsightedness, and the economic inequalities that force the world's poor to bear the brunt of an imbalanced system. And work in philosophy and history by scholars such as French philosopher Bruno Latour;[15] Mike Hulme, human geography professor at the University of Cambridge;[16] Dipesh Chakrabarty, professor of history at the University of Chicago;[17] and others has explored how this new epoch breaks down the age-old distinction between nature and society, between natural history and human history, and gives rise to new approaches to issues of justice: "justice between generations, between small island-nations and the polluting countries (both past and prospective), between developed, industrialized nations (historically responsible for most emissions) and the newly industrialized ones."[18] With such new thinking comes the opportunity to reconsider Enlightenment ideas such as "freedom, choice, morality, citizenship, difference and rights."[19]

Certainly business will be an important force in the emergence of this future scenario. But it will require new kinds of enlightened leadership that recognize the need for deep systemic change within the market. This change will begin with a recognition of the need for regulation to establish a balanced set of rules to guide market activity. These rules will be developed by moving beyond the stale debates over too much or too little government and instead toward the right kind of government engagement with the market. Further, it will require a shift in commonly negative notions of lobbying as corrupting the regulatory process through self-interested gamesmanship and instead will consider a relationship between business and the government that promotes the common good.

This will lead to shifting notions of the role of the corporation in serving society and the role of the executive in running it. We can see the beginnings of those shifts today, as BlackRock, the Business Roundtable, and the World Economic Forum issue such statements as "the purpose of a corporation" is far more than serving shareholders;[20] public companies have a responsibility not only to deliver profits but also to make "a positive contribution to society";[21] and the corporation "serves society at large . . . pays its fair share of taxes . . . [and] acts as a steward of the environmental and material universe for future generations."[22] The next step is for these notions to become manifest in action and diffused throughout the business environment.

Production processes, for example, will become circular in nature, eliminating both the use of virgin materials and the disposal of waste. The economy will grow while decreasing the amount of materials and energy needed to achieve that growth. Mobility solutions will be developed that do not require more cars. Communication processes will be fully transparent, such that all corporate activities (such as political lobbying, workplace conditions, fair wages paid, environmental impacts) are visible to those who can evaluate their efficacy. Marketing tools and capabilities will be used to inform consumers on the collective social and environmental impacts of their individual consuming choices. Organizations will be designed to include employees (such as ESOPs), the community (such as COOPs), social and environmental considerations (such as Benefit Corporations), or others. Human resource protocols, job design, and reward systems will help employees flourish and gain greater meaning and purpose through their work. New accounting standards and finance models will incorporate social and environmental considerations in harmony with economic metrics. Ultimately, we will rethink the basic ideas of growth and consumption by developing new mechanisms by which services are provided and profits are derived, and disconnecting revenues from materials, energy, or human exploitation.

### SHAPING YOUR FUTURE

As we consider the possibilities of our future, the market and business are both the cause and the possible solution to our Anthropocene challenges. Therefore, the role that you take within business has tremendous import for the kind of world you will leave to future generations. What world will that be? Our future society may become chaotic as in Collapsing Systems, or it may become more mindful as in Re-Enlightenment. Humans certainly have the capacity to respond to the unprecedented social and environmental challenges we face, as we did with reversing ozone depletion (scientists predict that the ozone hole will close completely by mid-century).[23] But future adaptations will depend on forethought, care, and wisdom. To get there, business must be part of the solution, and you as a business leader must guide it there.

The responsibility we face to steward our social and planetary ecosystems represents the great challenge of today's generation, and possibly the greatest challenge of any generation. Environmental theologian Thomas Berry has called such a challenge *The Great Work*, and the sentiment in this passage captures the challenge before us:

> The success or failure of any historical age is the extent to which those living at that time have fulfilled the special role that history has imposed upon them. . . . We did not choose. We were chosen by some power beyond ourselves for this historical task. . . . We are, as it were, thrown into existence with a challenge and a role that is beyond any personal choice. The nobility of our lives, however, depends upon the manner in which we come to understand and fulfill our assigned role.[24]

In the early 1940s, many business students had to put aside their dreams of Wall Street or finance for the great work of World War II. And the nobility of that generation was measured by how well that generation came to understand and fulfill their assigned role. To my mind, the great work for today's generation lies in correcting the flaws in capitalism that lead to the systemic breakdowns that issues like climate change and income inequality expose.

You, the next generation of business leaders, have been born into this reality, and you have no choice but to respond. You did not choose this reality but you must embrace it. The nobility of your lives will be determined by how you respond to the challenges you face. And today's business schools will be judged by how well they prepare you to meet that challenge. If they fall short in that effort, you must take responsibility for your education and amend it to fit your times, your challenges, and your vocation.

# ACKNOWLEDGMENTS

I extend my deepest thanks to Geoff Dembicki for his editorial help in the development of this book, pushing me to draw out deeper ideas, polishing the text, and helping me to tie the ideas together into a consistent and cohesive manuscript. As a journalist focused on climate change, politics, and business, his content knowledge helped in tightening and expanding my examples. As an editor, his clarifying eye has made this a far better book. I would also like to thank some of my academic coauthors with whom I developed some of the thinking that went into this book: my former adviser, coauthor, and continual mentor, John Ehrenfeld; two more recent coauthors, Ellen Hughes-Cromwick at the University of Michigan and Todd Schifeling at Temple University; and Dev Jennings at the University of Alberta, with whom I have had one of the most productive collaborative relationships of my academic career. Finally, I would like to thank the many editors who have supported a lot of the thinking and writing that preceded this book: Martin LaMonica, Bryan Keogh, and Bruce Wilson at *The Conversation*; Eric Nee, Marcie Bianco, and David Johnson at the *Stanford Social Innovation Review*; Cameron French and Evan Nesterak at *Behavioral Scientist*; Rebecca Marsh at Greenleaf Publishing; Margaret Krebs and Pam Sturner at *Leopold Leadership* 3.0; P. J. Simmons at the Corporate Eco-Forum; James Vansteel at the *Michigan Journal of Public Affairs*; Erik Assadourian at the Worldwatch Institute; and Steve Catalano, my editor at Stanford University Press.

# ABOUT THE AUTHOR

**ANDREW J. HOFFMAN** is the Holcim (US) Professor at the University of Michigan, a position that holds joint appointments in the Stephen M. Ross School of Business and the School for Environment and Sustainability. He writes about the processes by which environmental and social issues both emerge and evolve as social, political, and managerial considerations. He has published over one hundred articles and book chapters, as well as sixteen books, which have been translated into five languages. He earned his PhD in both Management and Civil & Environmental Engineering at MIT and lives with his wife, journalist and writer Joanne Will, in Ann Arbor, Michigan.

# NOTES

**FOREWORD**

1. A. Guterres, "Remarks at 2019 Climate Action Summit," September 23, 2019, https://www.un.org/sg/en/content/sg/speeches/2019-09-23/remarks-2019-climate-action-summit.

2. G. Thunberg, "If world leaders choose to fail us, my generation will never forgive them," *The Guardian*, September 23, 2019.

3. Deloitte, *The Deloitte global millennial survey 2019: Societal discord and technological transformation create a "generation disrupted,"* 2019, https://www2.deloitte.com/content/dam/Deloitte/global/Documents/About-Deloitte/deloitte-2019-millennial-survey.pdf.

**CHAPTER 1: MANAGEMENT AS A CALLING**

1. P. J. Henning, "White collar crime sentences after Booker: Was the sentencing of Bernie Ebbers too harsh?" *McGeorge Law Review* 37 (2006): 757.

2. A. Ross Sorkin, "Ex-corporate lawyer's idea: Rein in 'sociopaths' in the boardroom," *New York Times*, July 29, 2019.

3. J. Gamble, "The most important problem in the world," *Medium*, March 13, 2019.

4. M. Benioff, "We need a new capitalism," *New York Times*, October 14, 2019.

5. J. Stiglitz, "Progressive capitalism is not an oxymoron," *New York Times*, April 19, 2019.

6. J. Benjamin, "Business class: The bankrupt ideology of business school," *The New Republic*, May 14, 2018.

7. S. Long, "The financialization of the American elite," *American Affairs* (Fall 2019).

8. D. McDonald, "When you get that wealthy, you start to buy your own bullshit: The miseducation of Sheryl Sandberg," *Vanity Fair*, November 27, 2018.

9. M. Parker, "Why we should bulldoze the business school," *The Guardian*, April 27, 2018.

10. C. Doherty, J. Kiley, and B. Johnson, *The partisan divide on political values grows even wider* (Washington, DC: Pew Research Center, 2017).

11. B. Lillian, "DOE report confirms wind energy costs at all-time lows," *North American Windpower*, August 15, 2019.

12. G. Kavlak, J. McNerney, and J. Trancik, "Evaluating the causes of cost reduction in photovoltaic modules," *Energy Policy* 123 (2018): 700–710.

13. Center for Climate and Energy Solutions, *Renewable energy*, 2018, https://www.c2es.org/content/renewable-energy.

14. J. Hootkin and T. Meck, *Call to action in the age of Trump* (New York: Business Strategy Group, 2018).

15. "The MBA Oath," http://mbaoath.org.

16. A. Hoffman, "Management as a calling," *Stanford Social Innovation Review*, September 4, 2018.

17. Gamble, "Most important problem in the world."

18. N. Maxwell, *From knowledge to wisdom: A revolution for science and the humanities* (London, UK: Pentire Press, 2007).

19. R. Ackoff, "From data to wisdom." *Journal of Applied Systems Analysis* 16, no. 1 (1989): 3–9.

20. N. Leiber, "Business students are putting planet over profits," *Bloomberg*, November 4, 2019.

21. Yale University/WBCSD, *Rising leaders on environmental sustainability and climate change: A global survey of business students* (New Haven, CT: Yale University Center for Business and the Environment, 2015).

22. Net Impact, *Business as unusual: The social and environmental impact guide to graduate programs—For students by students* (San Francisco: Net Impact, 2014).

23. A. Jack, "The rise of the 'sustainable' MBA," *Financial Times*, January 21, 2020; Jonathan Moules, "MBA students seek higher 'purpose' than mere money," *Financial Times*, October 20, 2019.

24. A. Hoffman, "The evolving focus of business sustainability education," in *State of the world. Earth ed: Rethinking education on a changing planet* (Washington, DC: Island Press, 2017): 279–288.

25. Benjamin, "Business class."

26. Quoted in S. Murray, "MBA teaching urged to move away from focus on shareholder primacy model," *Financial Times*, July 7, 2013.

27. W. Deresiewicz, *Excellent sheep: The miseducation of the American elite and the way to a meaningful life* (New York: Free Press, 2014).

28. Allbusinessschools.com, *MBA salary: What you can earn*, 2019, https://www.allbusinessschools.com/mba/salary.

29. B. Tuttle, "Here's how much you'll make at McKinsey, Bain and BCG in the U.S.," *efinancialcareers.com*, August 13, 2019.

30. S. Nasiripour, "Top U.S. B-school students pile on debt to earn MBAs," *Bloomberg*, June 17, 2019.

31. M. Travers, "The student debt crisis is crushing entrepreneurship," *Forbes*, October 17, 2019.

32. A. Hoffman, *Finding purpose: Environmental stewardship as a personal calling* (Leeds, UK: Greenleaf, 2016).

33. Parker, "Why we should bulldoze the business school."

34. T. Edsall, "What does Tucker Carlson know that the Republican Party doesn't?" *New York Times*, February 6, 2019.

35. E. Beinhocker and N. Hanauer, "Redefining capitalism," *McKinsey Quarterly*, 3rd quarter (2014): 160–169.

36. L. Stout, "The problem with corporate purpose," *Brookings Institution Issues in Governance Studies* 48, no. 1 (2012).

37. F. Guerrera, Welch condemns share price focus," *Financial Times*, May 12, 2009.

38. P. Drucker, *The practice of management* (New York: HarperCollins, 1954).

39. S. Golden, "Barack Obama on climate, equity and overconsumption," *Green Biz*, November 26, 2019.

40. S. Woolfe and H. Shoomaker, "Life expectancy and mortality rates in the United States, 1959–2017," *Journal of the American Medical Association* 322, no. 20 (2019): 1996–2016.

41. Stiglitz, "Progressive capitalism is not an oxymoron."

42. C. Espana, I. Robinson, H. Bukhari, and D. Hodge, *Intel: Undermining the conflict mineral industry*, Case study #1-429-411 (Ann Arbor, MI: WDI, 2015).

43. Center for Climate and Energy Solutions, *Business support for the Paris Agreement*, 2018, https://www.c2es.org/content/business-support-for-the-paris-agreement.

44. L. Light, "Why U.S. businesses said 'stay in the Paris accord,'" CBS News, June 2, 2017.

45. D. Yaffe-Bellany, "Shareholder value is no longer everything, top CEOs say," *New York Times*, August 19, 2019.

46. K. Schwab, *Davos manifesto 2020: The universal purpose of a company in the fourth industrial revolution* (Davos, Switzerland: World Economic Forum, 2020).

47. A. Gupta, *The decade to deliver: A call to business action*, Accenture/United Nations Global Compact, 2019.

48. M. Rudolph, *12th annual survey of emerging risks* (Schaumburg, IL: Society of Actuaries, 2019).

49. H. Bottemiller Evich, "How a closed-door meeting shows farmers are waking up on climate change," *Politico*, December 9, 2019.

50. Aspen Institute, *Beyond grey pinstripes 2011–2012, Top 100 MBA programs* (New York: Aspen Institute, 2012).

51. T. Hart, C. Fox, K. Ede, and J. Korstad, "Do, but don't tell: The search for social responsibility and sustainability in the websites of the top-100 US MBA programs," *International Journal of Sustainability in Higher Education* 16, no. 5 (2015): 706–728.

52. Aspen Institute, "These business professors have ideas worth teaching," May 12, 2018, https://www.aspeninstitute.org/blog-posts/business-professors-ideas-worth-teaching.

53. *Larry Fink's 2019 letter to CEOS: Purpose & profit*, https://www.blackrock.com/corporate/investor-relations/larry-fink-ceo-letter.

54. G. Dembicki, "Wall Street's sustainable darling is profiting from climate change," *Vice*, May 24, 2019.

55. S. J. Gould, *The flamingo's smile: Reflections in natural history* (New York: Penguin, 1991).

56. M. Porter and C. van der Linde, "Green and competitive: Ending the stalemate," *Harvard Business Review* (September-October 1995): 120–134.

57. A. Giridharadas, *Winners take all: The elite charade of changing the world* (New York: Alfred A. Knopf, 2018).

58. G. James, "Why Unilever stopped issuing quarterly reports," *Inc.*, January 23, 2018.

59. R. Davies, "Norway's $1tn wealth fund to divest from oil and gas exploration," *The Guardian*, March 8, 2019.

60. E. Krukowska, "EU bank takes 'quantum leap' to end fossil-fuel financing," *Renewable Energy World*, November 15, 2019.

61. V. Volcovici, "Philanthropies, including Rockefellers, and investors pledge $50 billion fossil fuel divestment," *Scientific American*, September 22, 2014.

62. Board of Governors of the Federal Reserve System, *Report on the economic well-being of U.S. households in 2017*, 2018, https://www.federalreserve.gov/publications/files/2017-report-economic-well-being-us-households-201805.pdf.

63. E. Martin, "The government shutdown spotlights a bigger issue: 78% of US workers live paycheck to paycheck," CNBC, January 9, 2019.

64. M. Ross and N. Bateman, "Low unemployment isn't worth much if the jobs barely pay," Brookings Institution, January 8, 2020.

65. C. Morris, "42% of Americans have less than $10,000 saved for retirement," *Fortune*, April 18, 2018.

66. D. F. Wallace, "This is water," commencement speech at Kenyon College, 2005, https://fs.blog/2012/04/david-foster-wallace-this-is-water.

67. D. Brooks, *The second mountain: The quest for a moral life* (New York: Random House, 2019): 199.

## CHAPTER 2: THE CHANGING CONTEXT OF BUSINESS

1. A. Hoffman, *From heresy to dogma: An institutional history of corporate environmentalism* (Stanford, CA: Stanford University Press, 2001).

2. P. Lacy, T. Cooper, R. Hayward, and L. Neuberger *A new era of sustainability: UN global compact-Accenture CEO study* (New York: Accenture Institute for High Performance, 2010).

3. A. Gupta, *The decade to deliver: A call to business action*, Accenture/United Nations Global Compact, 2019.

4. Yaffe-Bellany, "Shareholder value is no longer everything."

5. *Larry Fink's 2019 letter to CEOS: Purpose & profit.*

6. Schwab, *Davos manifesto 2020.*

7. P. Crutzen, "Geology of mankind," *Nature* 415 (2002): 23; P. Crutzen and E. Stoermer, "The 'Anthropocene,'" *Global Change Newsletter* 41 (2000): 17–18.

8. Millennium Ecosystem Assessment, *Ecosystems and human well-being: Synthesis report* (Washington DC: Island Press, 2005).

9. J. Watts, "We have 12 years to limit climate change catastrophe, warns UN," *The Guardian*, October 8, 2018.

10. K. Epstein, "We can fix global warming, says the voice of 'Planet Earth.' But humans must hurry," *Washington Post*, January 22, 2019.

11. J. Moore, ed., *Anthropocene or Capitalocene? Nature, history, and the crisis of capitalism* (Oakland, CA: PM Press, 2016).

12. W. Steffen, P. Crutzen, and J. McNeil, "The Anthropocene: Are humans overwhelming the great forces of nature?" *AMBIO* 36 no. 8 (2007): 614–621.

13. F. Krausmann, S. Gingrich, N. Eisenmenger, K. Erb, H. Haberl, and M. Fischer-Kowalski, "Growth in global materials use, GDP and population during the 20th century." *Ecological Economics* 68 no. 10 (2009): 2696–2705.

14. Quoted in S. Stoll, "Fear of fallowing: The specter of a no-growth world," *Harper's Magazine*, March 2008.

15. S. Fidler, "Environmental risks loom large among World Economic Forum members," *Wall Street Journal*, January 15, 2020.

16. J. Ewing, "Climate change could cause the next financial meltdown," *New York Times*, January 23, 2020.

17. B. Morgan, "50 travel companies trying their hardest to reduce their carbon footprint," *Forbes*, August 5, 2019.

18. "Microsoft makes 'carbon negative' pledge," BBC News, January 16, 2020.

19. G. Lipton, "IKEA assembles plan to be carbon negative by 2030," *Landscape News*, January 17, 2020.

20. C. Clifford, "Tesla's Elon Musk: Uber Airbnb-type sharing of electric, self-driving cars is the 'obvious' future," *CNBC Make It*, May 3, 2018.

21. Quoted in R. Safian, "Ford CEO Jim Hackett on the future of car ownership and driving," *Fast Company*, January 9, 2018.

22. K. Korosec, "Bill Ford: Here's where Ford Motor Co. will be in 5 years," *Fortune*, May 17, 2016.

23. M. Barnard, "What will car ownership look like in the future?" *Forbes*, June 22, 2017.

24. US Department of Energy, *Vision of the Future Grid*, https://www.energy.gov/doe-grid-tech-team/vision-future-grid.

25. D. Shanker, L. Mulvany, and M. Hytha, "Beyond Meat just had the best IPO of 2019 as value soars to $3.8 billion," *Bloomberg*, May 2, 2019.

26. S. Samuel, "The many places you can buy Beyond Meat and Impossible Foods, in one chart," *Vox*, October 10, 2019.

27. A. Knapp, "Farming the next big food source: Crickets," *Forbes*, January 30, 2018.

28. D. Carrington, "Most 'meat' in 2040 will not come from dead animals, says report," *The Guardian*, June 12, 2019.

29. Patagonia Common Threads, https://www.patagonia.com/blog/2011/09/introducing-the-common-threads-initiative.

30. D. Lear, "Eliminating ocean plastic pollution must be a commercial and global priority," *The National*, November 14, 2018.

## CHAPTER 3: TRANSFORMING THE MARKET

1. A. Hoffman, "The next phase of business sustainability," *Stanford Social Innovation Review*, 2018, 34–39.

2. M. Porter and C. van der Linde, "Toward a new conception of the environment-competitiveness relationship," *Journal of Economic Perspectives* 94 (1995): 97–118.

3. S. Schmidheiny, *Changing course: A global business perspective on development and the environment*, (Cambridge, MA: MIT Press, 1992).

4. C. Holliday, S. Schmidheiny, and P. Watts, *Walking the talk: The business case for sustainable development* (San Francisco: Berrett-Koehler, 2002).

5. A. Hoffman, *Getting ahead of the curve: Corporate strategies that address climate change* (Arlington, VA: The Pew Center on Global Climate Change, 2006).

6. R. Reeves, "Capitalism used to promise a better future. Can it still do that?," *The Guardian*, May 22, 2019.

7. P. Farrell, "Myth of perpetual growth is killing America," *Wall Street Journal*, June 12, 2012.

8. N. Klein, "Capitalism killed our climate momentum, not 'human nature,'" *The Intercept*, August 3, 2018.

9. J. Ehrenfeld, *Sustainability by design* (New Haven, CT: Yale University Press, 2008).

10. A. Hoffman, "Capitalism must evolve to solve the climate crisis," *The Conversation* (US), September 16, 2015.

11. J. Ehrenfeld and A. Hoffman, *Flourishing: A frank conversation on sustainability* (Stanford, CA: Stanford University Press, 2013).

12. Q. Hardy, "Google says it will run entirely on renewable energy in 2017," *New York Times*, December 6, 2016.

13. J. Margolis, "Michelin isn't reinventing the wheel, it's reinventing the rubber supply chain," *PRI International*, August 24, 2016.

14. D. Kesmodel, J. Bunge, and B. MacKay, "Meat companies go antibiotics-free as more consumers demand it," *Wall Street Journal*, November 3, 2014.

15. Tyson Foods press release, *Tyson foods unveils alternative protein products and new Raised & Rooted® brand*, June 13, 2019.

16. N. Stern, *The economics of climate change: The Stern review*, (Cambridge, UK: Cambridge University Press, 2007).

17. A. Cifuentes and D. Espinoza, "Infrastructure investing and the peril of discounted cash flow," *Financial Times*, November 3, 2016.

18. N. Aslam, "Dow Jones continues its coronavirus stock market rally; Netflix stock plunges after its earnings," *Forbes*, July 17, 2020.

19. A. Tappe, "US economy posts its worst drop on record," *CNN Business*, July 30, 2020.

20. R. Kochhar, "Unemployment rose higher in three months of COVID-19 than it did in two years of the Great Recession," Pew Research Center Fact Tank, June 11, 2020.

21. K. Ehrhardt-Martinez, "Social determinants of deforestation in developing countries: A cross-national study," *Social Forces* 77, no. 2 (1998): 567–586.

22. J. Stiglitz, A. Sen, and J.-P. Fitoussi, *Mismeasuring our lives: Why GDP doesn't add up* (New York: New Press, 2010).

23. Ross School of Business, Center for Positive Organizations, https://positiveorgs.bus.umich.edu.

24. Weatherhead School of Management, Appreciative Inquiry, https://weatherhead.case.edu/core-topics/appreciative-inquiry.

25. A. Adams, D. Batista Rijo, B. Meza-Wilson, and B. Rolf, *Argus Farm Stop: Can a low-profit LLC be scaled to save the family farm*, Case study #1-543-605 (Ann Arbor, MI: WDI Publishing, 2019).

26. WBCSD, *A vision for sustainable consumption* (Geneva, Switzerland: World Business Council for Sustainable Development, 2011).

27. Associated Press, "Nestlé admits to forced labour in its seafood supply chain in Thailand," *The Guardian*, November 24, 2015.

28. E. Kolbert, *The sixth extinction: An unnatural history* (New York: Henry Holt, 2014).

29. Hoffman, "The next phase of business sustainability."

## CHAPTER 4: ADDRESSING CLIMATE CHANGE

1. A. Hoffman, "Rising insurance costs may convince Americans that climate change risks are real," *The Conversation*, October 22, 2018.

2. Executive Forum on Business and Climate, https://ncics.org/ncics/pdfs/events/forum/brochure-2013.pdf.

3. G. Dembicki, "The multi-billion dollar 'climate services' industry is altering access to climate change data: Critics fear some may lose out," *ensia*, August 2, 2019.

4. Quoted in A. Hoffman et al., *Academic engagement in public and political discourse: Proceedings of the Michigan meeting, May 2015* (Ann Arbor, MI: Michigan Publishing, 2015).

5. Munich Re, *Natural catastrophe review: Series of hurricanes makes 2017 year of highest insured losses ever*, Munich Re, January 4, 2018.

6. H. Fountain, J. Patel, and N. Popovich, "2017 was one of the hottest years on record. And that was without El Niño," *New York Times*, January 13, 2018.

7. D. Jergler, "Report outlines climate change risks faced by insurance sector," *Insurance Journal*, August 23, 2018.

8. P. Domm, "Hurricane Florence damage estimated at $17 billion to $22 billion and could go higher—Moody's Analytics," CNBC, September 17, 2018.

9. H. Pike, "Report: Camp Fire world's costliest natural disaster in 2018, damage cost of $16.5 billion," WRCR News, January 8, 2019.

10. E. Faust and M. Steuer, "New hazard and risk level for wildfires in California and worldwide," Munich Re, 2019, https://www.munichre.com/content/dam/munichre/global/content-pieces/documents/Whitepaper%20wildfires%20and%20climate%20change_2019_04_02.pdf.

11. L. S. Howard, "Natural catastrophe claims in 2017 reached a record $135B: Munich Re," *Insurance Journal*, January 4, 2018.

12. G. Dembicki, "The $1 trillion storm: How a single hurricane could rupture the world economy," *Vice*, March 3, 2019.

13. Quoted in A. Neslen, "Climate change could make insurance too expensive for most people—report," *The Guardian*, March 21, 2019.

14. B. Hulac, "Climate change goes firmly in the "loss" column for insurers," *E&E News*, March 15, 2018.

15. D. Caplinger, "Why hurricanes don't worry Warren Buffett," *The Motley Fool*, March 16, 2018.

16. CERES, *Insurer climate risk disclosure survey: 2012 findings & recommendations* (Boston: CERES, 2013).

17. D. Jergler, "Insurance industry making 'significant contributions' in climate change battle, report shows," *Insurance Journal*, January 25, 2018.

18. Insurance Journal Research, *Climate change risks to the insurance sector*, August 27, 2018, https://www.insurancejournal.com/research/research/climate-change-risks-to-the-insurance-sector.

19. M. Rudolph, *12th annual survey of emerging risks*, (Schaumburg, IL: Society of Actuaries, 2019).

20. B. Hope and N. Friedman, "Climate change is forcing the insurance industry to recalculate," *Wall Street Journal*, October 3, 2018.

21. T. Kuykendall, "Liberty Mutual to stop insuring thermal coal projects," *Institute for Energy Economics and Financial Analysis*, December 16, 2019.

22. E. Sulakshana, "First major US insurer begins divestment from fossil fuels," *EcoWatch*, September 12, 2019.

23. R. K. Beals, "Goldman Sachs becomes first major US bank to stop funding Arctic drilling, pulls back from coal," *MarketWatch*, December 21, 2019.

24. P. Bartolone, "Their home survived the Camp Fire—but their insurance did not," NPR, February 17, 2019.

## CHAPTER 5: RETHINKING BUSINESS-
## GOVERNMENT ENGAGEMENT

1. A. Ross Sorkin, "Paul Volcker, at 91, sees 'a hell of a mess in every direction,'" *New York Times*, October 23, 2018.

2. Gallup, *Congress and the public*, 2017, https://news.gallup.com/poll/1600/congress-public.aspx.

3. F. Newport, "Americans want more than just budget cuts," Gallup, June 9, 2017.

4. C. Doherty, J. Kiley, A. Tyson, and B. Jameson, *Beyond distrust: How Americans view their government* (Washington, DC: Pew Research Center, 2015).

5. J. Norman, "Americans worry less about government regulation," Gallup, October 11, 2018.

6. A. Swift, "Americans' views on government regulation remain steady," Gallup, October 11, 2017.

7. C. Doherty, J. Kiley, and B. Johnson, *The partisan divide on political values grows even wider* (Washington, DC: Pew Research Center, 2017).

8. E. Ekins, *Wall Street vs. the regulators: Public attitudes on banks, financial regulation, consumer finance, and the Federal Reserve* (Washington, DC, Cato Institute, 2017).

9. K. Bowman, "Where is the public on government regulation?" *Forbes*, October 23, 2018.

10. M. Gilens and B. Page, "Testing theories of American politics: Elites, interest groups, and average citizens," *Perspectives on Politics* 12 no. 3 (2014): 564–581.

11. K. Evers-Hillstrom, "Lobbying spending reaches $3.4 billion in 2018, highest in 8 years," *Open Secrets*, January 25, 2019.

12. Open Secrets, 2018 *outside spending, by race*, 2020.

13. A. He, "Election 2018: How big business spent its money," *The Northwestern Business Review*, November 7, 2018.

14. InfluenceMap, *Big oil's real agenda on climate change*, 2019, https://influencemap .org/report/How-Big-Oil-Continues-to-Oppose-the-Paris-Agreement-38212275958aa 21196dae3b76220bddc.

15. K. Peterson and M. Pfitzer, "Lobbying for good," *Stanford Social Innovation Review*, Winter 2009.

16. T. Lyon, M. Delmas, and J. Maxwell, "CSR needs CPR: Corporate sustainability and politics," *California Management Review*, June 6, 2018.

17. Exxon Mobil position on climate change, https://corporate.exxonmobil.com/ en/Energy-and-environment/Environmental-protection/Climate-change.

18. S. Laville, "Top oil firms spending millions lobbying to block climate change policies, says report," *The Guardian*, March 21, 2019.

19. T. Lyon and M. Delmas, "When corporations take credit for green deeds their lobbying may tell another story," *The Conversation* (US), July 17, 2019.

20. Y. Mounk, "America is not a democracy: How the United States lost the faith of its citizens—and what it can do to win them back," *The Atlantic*, March, 2018.

21. J. McGregor, "Corporate America's embrace of gay rights has reached a stunning tipping point," *Washington Post*, April 5, 2016.

22. B. Alpert, "Case of Jamal Khashoggi puts financial ties to Saudis under strain," *Barron's*, October 19, 2018.

23. J. Rubin, "Hobby Lobby's win for religious freedom," *Washington Post*, June 30, 2014.

24. S. Wolfson, "Ambien maker responds to Roseanne Barr: 'Racism is not a known side effect,'" *The Guardian*, May 30, 2018.

25. N. Smith, "Balancing social activism in the workplace," *The Buzz Bin*, January 15, 2019.

26. A. Hoffman, "The activist CEO," *Stanford Social Innovation Review*, Spring, 2020, 67–69.

27. M. Gardner, L. Roque, and S. Wamhoff, *Corporate tax avoidance in the first year of the Trump tax law* (Washington, DC: Institute on Taxation and Economic Policy, 2019).

28. A. Ross Sorkin, "How shareholder democracy failed the people, *New York Times*, August 20, 2019.

29. J. Taylor, "The alternative to ideology," Niskanen Center, October 29, 2018.

## CHAPTER 6: DEMOCRACY AND THE MARKETPLACE

1. A. Hoffman, "Democracy is giving way to the market, and ultimately to the mob. James Madison would be appalled," *Michigan Journal of Public Affairs*, April 15, 2019.

2. US Customs and Immigration Service, n.d., https://www.uscis.gov/system/files_force/USCIS/files/Government_and_You_handouts.pdf.

3. J. Bauer-Wolf, "Reclaiming their campuses," *Inside Higher Education*, March 21, 2018.

4. L. Rozsa and S. Svrluga, "Florida governor declares state of emergency in advance of Richard Spencer event," *Washington Post*, October 16, 2017.

5. B. McVicar, "Richard Spencer's Michigan State visit culminates with fights, anti-Nazi chants," *M Live*, January 30, 2019.

6. Ballotpedia, 2018 ballot measures, https://ballotpedia.org/2018_ballot_measures.

7. J. Woolfolk and K. Bartley, "More money spent to sway California voters on Nov. 6," *Daily Democrat*, October 31, 2018.

8. C. Horton, "Taiwan asked voters 10 questions. It got some unexpected answers." *New York Times*, November 26, 2018.

9. "National politics on Twitter: Small share of U.S. adults produce majority of tweets," Pew Research Center, October 23, 2019.

10. Z. Chong, "Up to 48 million Twitter accounts are bots, study says," C/Net, March 14, 2017.

11. A. Romano, "Two-thirds of links on Twitter come from bots. The good news? They're mostly bland," *Vox*, April 9, 2018.

12. B. Wolford, "Mob mentality: The brain suppresses personal moral code when in groups," *Medical Daily*, June 14, 2014.

13. M. Plata, "Is social media making us ruder? Research says a "lack of eye contact" is to blame." *Psychology Today*, February 26, 2018.

14. Ibid.

15. T. Avant, "Examining the mob mentality," *South Source*, January 2011.

16. J. Ronson, "How one stupid tweet blew up Justine Sacco's life," *New York Times*, February 12, 2015.

17. Quoted in A. Trafton, "When good people do bad things," *MIT News*, June 12, 2014.

18. Quoted in T. Bissell, "An anti-Facebook manifesto, by an early Facebook investor," *New York Times*, January 29, 2019.

19. J. Kavanaugh and M. Rich, *Truth decay: An initial exploration of the diminishing role of facts and analysis in American public life* (Santa Monica, CA: RAND Corporation, 2018).

## CHAPTER 7: LEARNING THE VALUE OF GOVERNMENT IN THE WAKE OF A SHUTDOWN

1. C. Cederlof, "Garbage, feces, other bad behavior take toll on national parks during shutdown," *USA Today*, January 1, 2019.

2. A. Halsey and M. Laris, "10 percent of TSA workers called out Sunday as shutdown continues," *Washington Post*, January 21, 2019.

3. A. Uzialko, "How a government shutdown hurts small businesses," *Business News Daily*, December 26, 2018.

4. C. Clark, "Everyone dreads shutdowns, so why do they keep happening?" *Government Executive*, July 18, 2019.

5. A. Hoffman and E. Hughes-Cromwick, "Shutdown's economic impact is a forceful reminder of why government matters," *The Conversation*, January 22, 2019.

6. Reuters, "Factbox: Departments hit by partial U.S. government shutdown," December 31, 2018.

7. "Federal government shutdown slows FDA inspections," *Occupational Health & Safety*, January 14, 2019.

8. B. Pisani, "This government shutdown is starting to get the IPO market nervous," CNBC, January 16, 2019.

9. A. Sparhawk, "Government shutdown frustrates craft breweries," CraftBeer.com, January 15, 2019.

10. M. Fox, "Government shutdown stops FDA food safety inspections," NBC News, January 9, 2019.

11. O. Milman, "'It's a nightmare': Americans' health at risk as shutdown slashes EPA," *The Guardian*, January 9, 2019.

12. J. Tankerlsey, "Shutdown's economic damage starts to pile up, threatening an end to growth," *New York Times*, January 15, 2019.

13. Y. Li, "If the shutdown lasts two more weeks, the cost to the economy will exceed price of Trump's wall," CNBC, January 11, 2019.

14. B. Adler, ed., *America's founding fathers: Their uncommon wisdom and wit* (London, UK: Rowman & Littlefield, 2015).

15. M. Lewis, *The fifth risk* (New York: W. W. Norton, 2018).

16. D. Graham-Rowe, "Fifty years of DARPA: A surprising history," *New Scientist*, May 15, 2008.

17. E. Stewart, "How close are we to another financial crisis? 8 experts weigh in," *Vox*, September 18, 2018.

18. A. Tanzi, "Global debt topped $247 trillion in the first quarter, IIF says," *Bloomberg*, July 10, 2018.

19. M. Krantz, "Stock market crash near? Nobel laureate sees 'bubbles everywhere,'" *Investor's Business Daily*, October 25, 2019.

20. J. Norman, "Americans worry less about government regulation," Gallup, October 11, 2018.

21. L. Qui, "Trump says 'no president has ever cut so many regulations.' Not quite." *New York Times*, February 23, 2018.

22. E. Ekins, *Wall Street vs. the regulators: Public attitudes on banks, financial regulation, consumer finance, and the federal reserve* (Washington, DC: Cato Institute, 2017).

23. Y. Levin, "Recovering the case for capitalism," *National Affairs*, Spring 2010.

24. J. Buntin, "25 years later, what happened to 'Reinventing Government'?" *Governing the States & Localities*, September 2016.

## CHAPTER 8: FIGHTING CLIMATE CHANGE TOGETHER

1. M. Taylor, M. Weaver, and H. Davidson, "IPCC climate change report calls for urgent action to phase out fossil fuels—as it happened," *The Guardian*, October 8, 2018.

2. A. Bennett, "NC banned a study on sea-level rise. Could it mean more hurricane destruction?" *News & Observer*, September 12, 2018.

3. T. Korten, "In Florida, officials ban term 'climate change,'" *Miami Herald*, March 8, 2015.

4. K. Sack and J. Schwartz, "As storms keep coming, FEMA spends billions in 'cycle' of damage and repair," *New York Times*, October 8, 2018.

5. A. Hoffman and E. Hughes-Cromwick, "Nobel award recognizes how economic forces can fight climate change," *The Conversation*, October 9, 2018.

6. W. Nordhaus, *The climate casino: Risk, uncertainty, and economics for a warming world* (New Haven, CT: Yale University Press, 2013).

7. F. Andrews, "'Climate Casino': An overview of global warming," *New York Times*, November 30, 2013.

8. W. Stevens, "How much is nature worth? For you, $33 trillion," *New York Times*, May 20, 1997, B7, B9.

9. National Bureau of Economic Research, *Integrated Assessment Models of Climate Change*, 2017, https://www.nber.org/reporter/2017number3/nordhaus.html.

10. W. Nordhaus, "The 'DICE' model: Background and structure of a dynamic integrated climate-economy model of the economics of global warming" (No. 1009), Cowles Foundation for Research in Economics, Yale University, 1992.

11. R. Murphy, "William Nordhaus versus the United Nations on climate change economics," *Library of Economics and Liberty*, November 5, 2018.

12. J. Stiglitz, "Progressive capitalism is not an oxymoron," *New York Times*, April 19, 2019.

13. K. Peterson and M. Pfitzer, "Lobbying for good," *Stanford Social Innovation Review*, Winter 2009.

## CHAPTER 9: COMMUNICATING IN POLITICALLY CHARGED ENVIRONMENTS

1. PwC, *22nd annual global CEO survey: CEOs' curbed confidence spells caution*, 2019, https://www.pwc.com/mu/pwc-22nd-annual-global-ceo-survey-mu.pdf.

2. E. Rosenbaum, "Here's what Warren Buffett thinks about climate change," CNBC, March 25, 2019.

3. A. Bullock and S. Trombley, eds., *The new Fontana dictionary of modern thought* (London: Harper Collins, 1999): 775.

4. T. Burnett, *What is Scientism?* American Association for the Advancement of Science, n.d., https://www.aaas.org/programs/dialogue-science-ethics-and-religion/what-scientism.

5. R. Brulle, "Institutionalizing delay: Foundation funding and the creation of US

climate change counter-movement organizations," *Climatic Change* 122, no. 4 (2014): 681–694.

6. Quoted in S. Goldenberg, "Secret funding helped build vast network of climate denial thinktanks," *The Guardian*, February 14, 2013.

7. A. Hoffman, "The culture and discourse of climate skepticism," *Strategic Organization* 9, no. 1 (2011): 77–84.

8. A. Hoffman, "Talking past each other? Cultural framing of skeptical and convinced logics in the climate change debate," *Organization & Environment* 24, no. 1 (2011): 3–33.

9. M. Ballew, J. Marlon, and A. Leiserowitz, "Explore climate change in the American mind," Yale Program on Climate Change Communication, April 13, 2019.

10. A. Hoffman, "Climate science as culture war," *Stanford Social Innovation Review*, Fall 2012.

## CHAPTER 10: WORLDVIEWS AND SOCIAL MOVEMENTS

1. C. Funk and B. Kennedy, "The politics of climate change," Pew Research Center, November 4, 2016.

2. D. Kahan, H. Jenkins-Smith, and D. Braman, "Cultural cognition of scientific consensus." *Journal of Risk Research* 14, no. 2 (2011): 147–174.

3. Y. Heath and R. Gifford, "Free-market ideology and environmental degradation: The case of belief in global climate change." *Environment and Behavior* 38, no. 1 (2006): 48–71.

4. J. Manzi and P. Wehner, "Conservatives and climate change," *National Affairs*, Summer 2015.

5. Governor's Office of Planning and Research, *Scientific organizations that hold the position that climate change has been caused by human action*, State of California, 2014, http://opr.ca.gov/s_listoforganizations.php.

6. Joint National Science Academies, *Joint Science Academies' statement: Global response to climate change*, 2005, http://nationalacademies.org/onpi/06072005.pdf.

7. T. Jacobs, "On climate, the GOP is an outlier," *Pacific Standard*, May 3, 2017.

8. A. Hoffman, "Breaking the link between a conservative worldview and climate skepticism," *The Conversation*, October 29, 2015.

9. J. Tures, "Even Republicans are aware that climate change is happening," *Observer*, July 10, 2019.

10. K. Ahmed, "Bank of England governor—global economy at risk from climate change," BBC News, September 29, 2015.

11. "Climate change: Central banks warn of financial risks in open letter," BBC News, April 17, 2019.

12. B. Thompson, "Cargill executive tells K-State crowd climate change threatens food production," KCUR 89.3, October 13, 2015.

13. S. Karnowski, "General Mills sets ambitious goal for greenhouse gas cuts," Associated Press, August 30, 2015.

14. J. Zimmerman, "Rush Limbaugh, esteemed logician, proves that if you believe in God you can't believe in climate change," *Grist*, August 13, 2013.

15. "Pope Francis on climate change: Time is of the essence," *Vatican News*, March 28, 2019.

16. S. Weissman, "Muslim leaders support Islamic declaration on climate change," *Deseret News*, August 18, 2015.

17. L. Rechtman, "Jewish leaders join together to thank Pope Francis for championing climate," *The Coalition on the Environment and Jewish Life*, September 21, 2015.

18. "Dalai Lama praises Pope's environment encyclical," *Catholic Herald*, June 29, 2015.

19. T. Cama, "11 Republicans vow to fight climate change," *The Hill*, September 17, 2015.

20. G. Dembicki, "DC's Trumpiest congressman says the GOP needs to get real on climate change," *Vice*, March 25, 2019.

21. L. Friedman, "In a switch, some Republicans start citing climate change as driving their policies," *New York Times*, April 30, 2019.

22. L. Friedman and M. Astor, "5 takeaways from the Democrats' climate town hall," *New York Times*, September 5, 2019.

23. C. Davenport, "Many conservative Republicans believe climate change is a real threat," *New York Times*, September 28, 2015.

24. E. Lehrer, "Climate change: It's time for a conservative alternative," R Street, August 30, 2013.

25. J. Blum, "Shell leaving conservative ALEC over climate change views," *Fuel Fix*, August 7, 2015.

26. C. Mooney, "Climate deniers are in retreat," *Washington Post*, April 6, 2015.

27. Friedman and Astor, "5 takeaways from the Democrats' climate town hall."

28. T. Randall, "Americans have never been so sure about climate change—even Republicans," *Bloomberg*, October 23, 2015.

29. B. Drake, "How Americans view the top energy and environmental issues," Pew Research Center Fact Tank, January 15, 2015.

30. A. Leiserowitz et al., *Politics & global warming, March* 2018 (New Haven, CT: Yale Center on Climate Change Communication, 2018).

31. Clear Path, *Republicans, Clean Energy, and Climate Change*, n.d.,https://assets.clearpath.org/2016/09/clearpath_survey_report.pdf.

32. A. Leiserowitz, E. Maibach, S. Rosenthal, J. Kotcher, M. Ballew, M. Goldberg, and A. Gustafson, "Climate change in the American mind: December 2018," Yale Program on Climate Change Communication, 2019.

33. J. Myers, "AccuWeather predicts 2018 wildfires will cost California total economic losses of $400 billion," *AccuWeather*, November 21, 2018.

34. G. Dembicki, "This is what it would take for Republicans to actually fight climate change," *Vice*, March 14, 2019.

35. Quoted in S. Lerner, "How a professional climate change denier discovered the lies and decided to fight for science," *The Intercept*, April 28, 2017.

36. G. Dembicki, "Even with Trump in office, the climate denial movement is quietly falling apart," *Vice*, August 13, 2019.

37. "Not all Republicans think alike about global warming," Yale Program on Climate Change Communication Climate Note, January 12, 2015.

38. S. Wong, "Huntsman: GOP can't become 'anti-science' party," *Politico*, August 11, 2011.

39. Joint Labor Union and CEO Statement on the Paris Agreement, December 2, 2019, https://www.unitedforparisagreement.com.

## CHAPTER 11: THE RADICAL FLANK AND
## THE CLIMATE CHANGE DEBATE

1. B. McKibben, "Global warming's terrifying new math," *Rolling Stone*, July 19, 2012.

2. M. Gunther, "The fossil fuel divestment movement is failing. Except it's not," www.Marcgunther.com, July 27, 2015.

3. T. Schifeling and A. Hoffman, "Bill McKibben's influence on U.S. climate change discourse: Shifting field-level debates through radical flank effects," *Organization & Environment*, 2017, doi.org/10.1177/1086026617744278.

4. T. Schifeling and A. Hoffman, "How Bill McKibben's radical idea of fossil-fuel divestment transformed the climate debate," *The Conversation*, December 11, 2017.

5. H. Haines, "Black radicalization and the funding of civil rights: 1957–1970." *Social Problems* 32, no. 1 (1984), 31–43.

6. U.S. EPA, *US EPA oral history interview #2: Russell Train* (Washington, DC: U.S. Government Printing Office, 1993).

7. J. McPhee, "Encounters with the archdruid I—An island," *The New Yorker*, March 27, 1971.

8. J. Berlau, *Eco-freaks: Environmentalism is hazardous to your health!* (Nashville, TN: Nelson Current, 2006): 210.

9. Schifeling and Hoffman, "Bill McKibben's influence on U.S. climate change discourse."

10. R. Partington, "Mark Carney tells global banks they cannot ignore climate change dangers," *The Guardian*, April 17, 2019.

11. S. Dubb, "Taking stock of the fossil fuel divestment movement," *Non-Profit Quarterly*, September 13, 2018.

12. Y. Cadon, "$11 trillion and counting," Financing the Future, 2019, https://financingthefuture.platform350.org/wp-content/uploads/sites/60/2019/09/FF_11Trillion-WEB.pdf.

## CHAPTER 12: A NEW DEMOGRAPHIC IN
## THE CLIMATE CHANGE DEBATE

1. F. Buttel, "Environmentalization: Origins, processes, and implications for rural social change," *Rural Sociology* 57, no. 1 (1992): 1–27.

2. R. Brulle, "Institutionalizing delay: Foundation funding and the creation of U.S. climate change counter-movement organizations," *Climatic Change* 122, no. 4 (2014): 681–694.

3. C. Alter, S. Haynes, and J. Worland, "2019 person of the year: Greta Thunberg," *Time*, December 11, 2019.

4. M. Ballew, J. Marlon, S. Rosenthal, A. Gustafson, J. Kotcher, E. Maibach, and A. Leiserowitz, "Do younger generations care more about global warming?" Yale Program on Climate Change Communication, June 11, 2019.

5. A. Deutsch, "Surge in young Republicans worried about the environment: Survey," *Reuters*, August 29, 2019.

6. D. Lawson, K. Stevenson, M. Peterson, S. Carrier, R. Strnad, and E. Seekamp, "Children can foster climate change concern among their parents," *Nature Climate Change* 9 (2019): 458–462.

7. A. Leiserowitz, E. Maibach, S. Rosenthal, J. Kotcher, M. Ballew, M. Goldberg, and A. Gustafson, "Climate change in the American mind: December 2018," Yale Program on Climate Change Communication, 2019.

**CHAPTER 13: BUILD A LOW-CARBON WORLD FROM A HIGH-CARBON LIFESTYLE**

1. M. Haas, "Google summit on climate change attended by stars in private jets, mega yachts slammed as 'hypocritical,'" Fox News, August 2, 2019.

2. J. Romm, "The stunning hypocrisy of JP Morgan and CEO Jamie Dimon on climate change," *Think Progress*, March 21, 2019.

3. A. Harder, "Behind the energy and climate change hypocrisy in all of us," *Axios*, September 16, 2019.

4. A. Hoffman, "Eco-authenticity: Advocating for a low carbon world while living a high carbon lifestyle," *The Conversation*, March 31, 2016.

5. A. Hoffman, *Finding Purpose*.

6. "DataBlog: Carbon emissions per person, by country," *The Guardian*, 2019, https://www.theguardian.com/environment/datablog/2009/sep/02/carbon-emissions-per-person-capita.

7. J. B. MacKinnon, "Why you trust David Suzuki," *Readers Digest Canada*, 2015, https://www.readersdigest.ca/culture/why-you-trust-david-suzuki.

8. E. Griswold, "Giving up carbon for Lent," *The New Yorker*, March 23, 2020.

9. D. Lamire, "If you are serious about climate change . . . stop attending conferences?" 2013, https://lemire.me/blog/2013/12/04/if-you-are-serious-about-climate-change-stop-attending-conferences.

10. W. Achten, J. Almeida, and B. Muys, "Carbon footprint of science: More than flying," *Ecological Indicators* 34 (2013): 352–355.

11. Academic Flying, Press release, *Flying less: Reducing academia's carbon footprint*, https://academicflyingblog.wordpress.com/2015/10/19/press-release-for-public-launch-of-petition-october-19-2015.

12. "'Flight shame' could halve growth in air traffic," BBC News, October 2, 2019.

13. L. Hickman, "Should we stop worrying about the environmental impact of flying?" *The Guardian*, January 31, 2013.

14. M. Bookchin, *Toward an ecological society* (Montreal: Black Rose Books, 1997).

15. Ehrenfeld and Hoffman, *Flourishing*.

16. Pope Francis, *Encyclical letter laudato si': On care for our common home*, 2015, http://w2.vatican.va/content/francesco/en/encyclicals/documents/papa -francesco_20150524_enciclica-laudato-si.html.

## CHAPTER 14: BRIDGE SOCIAL DIVISIONS

1. A. Chatterji and M. Toffel, "The new CEO activists," *Harvard Business Review*, January-February 2018.

2. J. Kaplan, "Boycott culture forces CEOs to walk tightrope in Trump era," *Bloomberg*, February 15, 2017.

3. C. Riback, "Joseph Stiglitz: Saving capitalism from itself," *Chris Riback's Conversations*, June 21, 2019.

4. S. Farrell, "'Damaged ideology': Business must reinvent capitalism—ex-Unilever boss," *The Guardian*, October 29, 2019.

5. D. Walker, "Ford Foundation's Darren Walker: How to save capitalism from itself," *Fast Company*, October 17, 2019.

6. R. Dalio, "The world has gone mad and the system is broken," *Linked In Influencer*, November 5, 2019.

7. Farrell, "'Damaged ideology.'"

8. M. Benioff, "We need a new capitalism," *New York Times*, October 14, 2019.

9. A. Hoffman, "How to bridge the political divide at the holiday dinner table," *The Conversation*, November 22, 2016.

10. A. Gustafson, P. Bergquist, A. Leiserowitz, and E. Maibach, "A growing majority of Americans think global warming is happening and are worried," Yale Program on Climate Change Communication, February 21, 2019.

11. T. Kuhn, *The structure of scientific revolutions*. (Chicago: Chicago University Press, 1962).

12. E. Romanelli and M. Tushman, "Organizational transformation as punctuated equilibrium: An empirical test," *Academy of Management Journal* 37, no, 5 (2017), https://doi.org/10.5465/256669.

13. J. Haidt, "Can a divided America heal?" TED Talk, November 2016.

14. M. Dimock, J. Kiley, S. Keeter, and C. Doherty, *Political polarization in the American public* (Washington, DC: Pew Research Center, 2014).

15. J. Herrman, "Fixation on fake news overshadows waning trust in real reporting," *New York Times*, November 18, 2016.

16. M. Bazerman and D. Moore, *Judgment in managerial decision making* (New York: John Wiley & Sons, 2012).

17. E. Pariser, *The filter bubble: How the new personalized web is changing what we read and how we think* (New York: Penguin Books, 2012).

18. M. Fisher and A. Taub, "How YouTube radicalized Brazil," *New York Times*, August 11, 2019.

19. *Partisanship and political animosity in* 2016 (Washington, DC: Pew Research Center, 2016).

20. T. Friedman, "Donald Trump, help heal the planet's climate change problem," *New York Times,* November 16, 2016.

21. M. Tanner, "Income inequality: Looking at the numbers," *National Review,* June 22, 2016.

22. G. White, "Stiglitz: Here's how to fix inequality," *The Atlantic,* November 2, 2015.

23. Gardner, Roque, and Wamhoff, *Corporate tax avoidance in the first year of the Trump tax law.*

24. N. Flannery, "Trump nation: Does income inequality now define the U.S. economy?" *Forbes,* August 15, 2016.

25. P. Dizikes, "The productive career of Robert Solow," *MIT News,* January-February 2020: 12.

26. R. Chetty et al., "The fading American dream: Trends in absolute income mobility since 1940," National Bureau of Economic Research, Working Paper No. 22910, 2016.

27. D. Howell, "From decent to lousy jobs: New evidence on the decline in American job quality, 1979–2017," Washington Center for Equitable Growth, August 30, 2019.

28. N. Kirsch, "The 3 richest Americans hold more wealth than bottom 50% of the country, study finds," *Forbes,* November 9, 2017.

29. L. Elliott, "World's 26 richest people own as much as poorest 50%, says Oxfam," *The Guardian,* January 20, 2019.

30. H. Zaidy, "The American Dream is much easier to achieve in Canada," *CNN Business,* January 20, 2020.

31. Friedman, "Donald Trump, help heal the planet's climate change problem."

**CHAPTER 15: CULTIVATE MULTIPLE WAYS OF KNOWING THE WORLD AROUND US**

1. J. Gamble, "The most important problem in the world," *Medium,* March 13, 2019.

2. K. Tippett, "Anand Giridharadas: When the market is our only language," *On Being,* November 15, 2018.

3. A. Hoffman, "Climate change and our emerging cultural shift," *Behavioral Scientist,* September 30, 2019.

4. A. Leopold, *A Sand County almanac: With other essays on conservation from Round River* (Oxford, UK: Oxford University Press, 1949).

5. D. Elgin, "Global warming and carbon dioxide ethics," *Huffington Post,* October 23, 2012.

6. B. Crossette, "Kofi Annan's astonishing facts," *New York Times,* September 27, 1998.

7. D. Kennedy, "The climate divide," *Science* 299, no. 5614 (2003): 1813.

8. A. Madrigal, "Kim Kardashian's private firefighters expose America's fault lines," *The Atlantic,* November 14, 2018.

9. A. Hoffman, "The limits of intellectual reason in our understanding of the natural world," *The Conversation,* June 1, 2016.

10. D. Brooks, *The second mountain: The quest for a moral life* (New York: Random House, 2019): 199.

11. W. Berry, *The unsettling of America: Culture & agriculture* (Berkeley, CA: Counterpoint Press, 1996).

12. T. Burnett, "What is Scientism?" American Association for the Advancement of Science, n.d., https://www.aaas.org/programs/dialogue-science-ethics-and-religion/what-scientism.

13. Ehrenfeld and Hoffman, *Flourishing*.

14. J. Haidt, *The righteous mind: Why good people are divided by politics and religion* (New York: Pantheon Books, 2012).

15. J. F. Kennedy, "Address at Rice University on the nation's space effort," September 12, 1962, John F. Kennedy Library, https://www.jfklibrary.org/archives/other-resources/john-f-kennedy-speeches/rice-university-19620912.

16. R. Gilruth, "I believe we should go to the moon," NASA, 1975, https://history.nasa.gov/SP-350/toc.html.

17. J. F. Kennedy, Commencement address at American University, June 10, 1963, John F. Kennedy Library, https://www.jfklibrary.org/archives/other-resources/john-f-kennedy-speeches/american-university-19630610.

## CHAPTER 16: THE FUTURE WORLD

1. A. Hoffman, "How driverless vehicles will redefine mobility and change car culture," *The Conversation*, February 24, 2016.

2. N. Boudette, "Despite high hopes, self-driving cars are 'way in the future,'" *New York Times*, July 17, 2019.

3. C. Chen, "What is the future of driverless cars?" *Christian Science Monitor*, November 15, 2015.

4. R. Siegel, "Secretary of Transportation: 'I see the future' when I'm in a self-driving car," *NPR All Things Considered*, February 22, 2016.

5. P. LeBeau, "Google gives more detail on safety of its autonomous cars," *MSNBC*, January 12, 2016.

6. A. Davies, "Model 3 crash testing hammers home Tesla's safety excellence," *Wired*, September 21, 2018.

7. S. Inskeep, "Remembering when driverless elevators drew skepticism," *NPR Planet Money*, July 31, 2015.

8. B. Lutz, "Bob Lutz: Kiss the good times goodbye," *Automotive News*, November 5, 2017.

9. A. Millard-Ball and L. Schipper, "Are we reaching peak travel? Trends in passenger transport in eight industrialized countries," *Transport Reviews* 31, no. 3 (2011): 357–378.

10. J. Weissmann, "Why don't young Americans buy cars?" *The Atlantic*, March 25, 2012.

11. S. Moss, "End of the car age: How cities are outgrowing the automobile," *The Guardian*, April 28, 2015.

12. P. Barter, "'Cars are parked 95% of the time.' Let's check!" *Reinventing Parking*, February 22, 2013.

13. A. Evans-Pritchard, "OPEC faces a mortal threat from electric cars," *The Telegraph*, December 23, 2015.

14. A. Lovins and H. Lovins, "Reinventing the wheels," *The Atlantic*, January 1995.

15. M. Fisher, "Cruising toward oblivion," *Washington Post*, September 2, 2015.

16. "Are your old vinyl records worth thousands? Here's how to sell them," *Flipsy*, n.d., https://flipsy.com/article/41/the-spin-on-the-vinyl-record-collection-market.

17. M1 Concourse, https://m1concourse.com.

18. U. Garcia, "Prosecutors in Yavapai County announced Tuesday that they didn't find evidence to criminally charge Uber in the crash," *AZ Central*, March 6, 2019.

19. T. Worstall, "Driverless trucks Armaggeddon: So, truck drivers will just go do something else," *Forbes*, May 28, 2015.

## CHAPTER 17: YOUR ROLE IN YOUR OWN FUTURE

1. D. Brooks, *The road to character* (New York: Penguin Books, 2015).

2. P. Eavis, "It's never been easier to be a C.E.O., and the pay keeps rising," *New York Times*, May 24, 2019.

3. W. R. Scott and G. Davis, *Organizations and organizing: Rational, natural and open systems perspectives* (Oxford, UK: Routledge, 2015).

4. A. Hoffman and P. D. Jennings, *Re-engaging with sustainability in the Anthropocene Era: An institutional approach* (Cambridge, UK: Cambridge University Press, 2018).

5. R. Khurana, *From higher aims to hired hands: The social transformation of American business schools and the unfulfilled promise of management as a profession* (Princeton, NJ: Princeton University Press, 2010).

6. A. Hoffman and P. D. Jennings, "How we respond to COVID-19 foreshadows future life in the Anthropocene," *Organizations and the Natural Environment Blog*, March 29, 2020.

7. A. Hoffman and P. D. Jennings, "Institutional-political scenarios for Anthropocene society," *Business & Society*, 2018, doi.org/10.1177/0007650318816468.

8. R. Scranton, "Lessons from a genocide can prepare humanity for climate apocalypse," *Technology Review*, April 24, 2019.

9. D. Wallace-Wells, *The Uninhabitable Earth: Life After Warming* (New York: Tim Duggan Books, 2019).

10. G. Shill, "Americans shouldn't have to drive, but the law insists on it," *The Atlantic*, July 9, 2019.

11. J. Maxwell and F. Briscoe, "There's money in the air: The CFC ban and DuPont's regulatory strategy," *Business Strategy and the Environment* 6, no. 5 (1997): 276–286.

12. L. Thévenot, M. Moody, and C. Lavaye, "Forms of valuing nature: Arguments and modes of justification in French and American environmental disputes," In *Rethinking comparative cultural sociology: Repertoires of evaluation in France and the United*

*States*, ed. L. Lamont and L. Thévenot, 229–272 (Cambridge, UK: Cambridge University Press, 2000).

13. N. Evernden, *The natural alien: Humankind and the environment*, (Toronto, Canada: University of Toronto Press, 1985).

14. R. Rowan, "Notes on politics after the Anthropocene," *Progress in Human Geography* 38, no. 3 (2014): 9–12.

15. B. Latour, "Agency at the time of the Anthropocene," *New Literary History* 45, no. 1 (2014): 1–18.

16. M. Hulme, "Reducing the future to climate: A story of climate determinism and reductionism," *Osiris* 26 (2011): 245–266.

17. D. Chakrabarty, "The climate of history: Four theses," *Critical Inquiry* 35, no. 2 (2009): 197–222.

18. D. Chakrabarty, "Climate and capital: On conjoined histories," *Critical Inquiry* 41, no. 1 (2014): 1–23.

19. A. Mikhail, "Enlightenment Anthropocene," *Eighteenth-Century Studies* 49, no. 2 (2016): 211–231.

20. Yaffe-Bellany, "Shareholder value is no longer everything."

21. *Larry Fink's 2019 letter to CEOS: Purpose & profit.*

22. Schwab, *Davos manifesto.*

23. E. Hand, "Ozone layer on the mend, thanks to chemical ban," *Science*, June 30, 2016.

24. T. Berry, *The great work: Our way into the future.* (New York: Bell Tower, 2000).

# INDEX

AAAS, *see* American Association for the
Advancement of Science
Accenture, 14, 21–22
Activist CEOs, 55, 84, 102–3, 112
Adelson, Sheldon, 53
Agency theory, 37–39
Agriculture: climate change and, 14, 23,
25; future of, 27; nitrogen pollution, 23;
retail outlets, 37. *See also* Food industry
Airbus, 99
Air travel, greenhouse gas emissions, 95, 96,
97, 98–100
ALEC, *see* American Legislative Exchange
Council
Amazon, 90
American Association for the Advancement
of Science (AAAS), 75
American Legislative Exchange Council
(ALEC), 54, 82, 84
American Petroleum Institute (API), 54
Anderson, Kevin, 98
Anthropocene: business strategies, 22,
27–28, 33, 112; cultural shifts, 100,
134–38; defined, 3, 22; need for col-
lective action, 113, 130–31; planetary
boundaries, 23, 24 (fig.); potential sce-
narios, 130–38. *See also* Climate change;
Sustainability
API, *see* American Petroleum Institute
Apple, 14, 102, 125
Argus Farm Stop, 37
Aspen Institute, 14
A.T. Kearney, 27
Attenborough, David, 23

Authenticity, 17, 101
Automobile industry: driverless cars, 123–
24, 126–27; executives, 1–2; future of,
26–27, 31, 113, 121–27; political power,
134; sustainability research, 35

B (benefit) corporations, 36–37, 136
Ball, Whitney, 77
Bank for International Settlements, 26
Banks, 13, 65, 66, 95. *See also* Central banks
Barr, Roseanne, 55
Benioff, Marc, 2, 102, 103
Benjamin, John, 3, 8
Berkshire Hathaway, 45, 73–74
Berry, Thomas, 137
Berry, Wendell, 115
Beyond Meat, 27
Bhutan, Gross Happiness Index, 36
BlackRock, 14, 15, 22, 55, 136
*Bloomberg*, 9, 83, 87, 103
Bolsonaro, Jair, 106
Bookchin, Murray, 100
Bowman, Kaitlyn, 52
BP, 31
Brazil, 106
Brooks, David, 17, 115, 128–29
Brower, David, 86–87
Brulle, Robert, 75
Buffett, Warren, 45, 73–74
Business: engagement with government,
12–13, 52–56, 70; forms of organization,
36–37; future changes, 136–37; long-
term planning, 26, 31; political influence,
52–56, 58–59, 109, 129; shareholder